No More Mindless Homework

Dear Readers,

Much like the diet phenomenon *Eat This, Not That*, this series aims to replace some existing practices with approaches that are more effective—healthier, if you will—for our students. We hope to draw attention to practices that have little support in research or professional wisdom and offer alternatives that have greater support. Each text is collaboratively written by authors representing research and practice. Section 1 offers a practitioner's perspective on a practice in need of replacing and helps us understand the challenges, temptations, and misunderstandings that have led us to this ineffective approach. Section 2 provides a researcher's perspective on the lack of research to support the ineffective practice(s) and reviews research supporting better approaches. In Section 3, the author representing a practitioner's perspective gives detailed descriptions of how to implement these better practices. By the end of each book, you will understand both what not to do, and what to do, to improve student learning.

It takes courage to question one's own practice—to shift away from what you may have seen throughout your years in education and toward something new that you may have seen few if any colleagues use. We applaud you for demonstrating that courage and wish you the very best in your journey from this to that.

Best wishes,

— *Nell K. Duke and Ellin Oliver Keene, series editors*

No More Mindless Homework

Mindless Homework

KATHY COLLINS

JANINE BEMPECHAT

HEINEMANN
Portsmouth, NH

Heinemann
361 Hanover Street
Portsmouth, NH 03801–3912
www.heinemann.com

Offices and agents throughout the world

© 2017 by Kathleen Collins and Janine Bempechat

"Dedicated to Teachers" is a trademark of Greenwood Publishing Group, Inc.

Library of Congress Cataloging-in-Publication Data

Names: Collins, Kathy, author. | Bempechat, Janine, author.
Title: No more mindless homework / Kathy Collins, Janine Bempechat.
Description: Portsmouth, NH : Heinemann, [2017] | Series: Not this but that |
    Includes bibliographical references.
Identifiers: LCCN 2016055918 | ISBN 9780325092812
Subjects: LCSH: Homework. | Study skills. | Education—Parent participation.
Classification: LCC LB1048 .C645 2017 | DDC 371.30281—dc23

LC record available at https://lccn.loc.gov/2016055918

Series editors: Nell K. Duke *and* Ellin Oliver Keene
Editor: Margaret LaRaia
Production editor: Sean Moreau
Cover design: Lisa Fowler
Cover photograph: Jim Arbogast/Phodisc/Getty Images/HIP
Interior design: Suzanne Heiser
Typesetter: Valerie Levy, Drawing Board Studios
Manufacturing: Veronica Bennett

Printed in the United States of America on acid-free paper
21 20 19 18 17 VP 1 2 3 4 5

CONTENTS

✦ ✦

Kathy Collins thanks all of the teachers, children, and families
who have shared their stories of
making, designing, and parenting homework.

✦ ✦ ✦

Janine Bempechat thanks Margarita Jimenez-Silva and Rebecca Goldstein,
who generously gave their time to read and provide very helpful
feedback on early drafts of her section.

✦ ✦

INTRODUCTION

NELL K. DUKE

Homework. The word alone evokes strong emotions from children, youth, parents, and teachers. For most teachers I know, this word sits right between *rock* and *hard place.* If you assign too much homework, you risk complaints, if not outright misery, from parents, students, and—because you feel the need to give feedback on all that homework—yourself. If you assign too little homework, you risk being seen as "soft" and lacking in rigor, and—because homework can feel like it helps you "cover" the curriculum—feeling further behind. And that just regards the issue of how much homework. Then there are all the complexities around *what kinds of* homework.

Ellin and I did not take lightly the decision to try to navigate the treacherous waters of homework, and we considered very carefully who could captain the ship. Kathy Collins and Janine Bempechat were perfect for the role. Teachers across the country have long admired Kathy's approach to the teaching of young children, an approach that is imbued with respect for children's thinking. Janine is a meticulous interpreter of research. She resists the dichotomous thinking and generalities that too often plague us. Is homework entirely bad? No. Is homework entirely good? No. Janine helps us understand, based on the research we have to date, what homework offers and what it doesn't, what kinds of homework seem promising, and what kinds of supports help children engage in homework productively.

I encourage you to read this book with attention to nuance and detail. This isn't a book to fly through, but one to read with care, ideally in conversation with others. There are gems in here that a quick read might miss. For example, in a paragraph in section 2, Janine shares a study on the effects of teaching students strategies for managing their homework, including setting goals, self-evaluating, self-monitoring, and planning.

Students who received this training from their teachers over the course of five weeks, as compared to students who did not, demonstrated improved time management, self-reflection, self-efficacy, effort, interest, and desire for mastery—wow! Janine offers a powerful reminder that we can't just assign homework, we need to teach students *how to do* homework.

In section 3, Kathy describes a scene in the classroom of fourth-grade teacher Kevin Moore. Students worked in small groups to discuss how they solved a math problem assigned for homework the night before. Kathy "went from group to group, growing more enchanted by the intensity of children's participation." She explains that, "Mr. Moore circulated, too, offering support and asking follow-up and go-deeper questions." Her description illustrates both that homework can provide a starting point for compelling in-class activity and that peer-to-peer interactions can be a productive—and time-saving—strategy for providing feedback on homework.

I am grateful to Kathy and Janine for offering so much rich detail in the book—and more broadly for taking on such a stormy topic. With their leadership, I believe you'll find your journey through this book to be smooth sailing.

NOT THIS

Assigning "Just Because"

KATHY COLLINS

It was the week before the start of the school, and Mrs. B., my son's first-grade teacher, had scheduled appointments to meet individually with all of the children in her class and to talk briefly with their caregivers about the year ahead.

Owen's school experiences up to that point had been filled with story, play, inquiry, and lots of time outdoors in both his preschool settings and his kindergarten classroom, so we were curious about how he would make the transition into first grade at a new school, given the heightened academic expectations that have become characteristic of young children's school days.

As Owen explored his new classroom, Mrs. B talked to us about various projects and plans she had for the year. Then, in a lowered voice, she said, "Except for reading each night, I don't assign homework." She paused for a moment as if to gauge our reactions. She said that some families are relieved to hear about her light homework policy, but others express concerns about it, worried that their children will fall behind.

There have been teacher- and parent-led movements to change homework policies at many schools. PS 116, a highly regarded New York City public school, gained national attention when homework assignments were abolished altogether, which was based on recommendations from a school leadership team comprised of parents and school staff. Educators and journalists from around the country contacted PS 116 to find out more about how and why they revised their homework policy. Meanwhile, reactions among the school community were predictably mixed. Some families threatened to transfer their children, and others were elated with the change.

Many elementary schools are reconsidering their homework policies, both in terms of the quantity assigned and the content of those assignments. Finding consensus is challenging because the topic of homework at the elementary school level is polarizing for those immediately involved and directly affected: teachers, families, and children.

To Assign or Not to Assign? That Is One of the Questions

There has always been a measure of controversy surrounding the practice of homework. In the early 1900s, Edward Bok, the editor of the influential *Ladies Home Journal,* wrote editorials and articles about the evils of homework, even calling it "a severe hazard to children's mental and physical health (Gill and Schlossman 1996)."

Fast forward to the mid-twentieth-century, and after involvement in two world wars as well as other military conflicts, the nation's outlook was different. The Soviet Union just launched Sputnik, the Cold War weighed heavily, and there was a growing worry about the international stature of the United States, in terms of geopolitical influence, economic power, and military dominance. These worries created a sense of national insecurity, and one of the responses was to blame and then demand more of our schools, including a call for more and harder homework, in efforts to increase the international competitiveness of the American student.

All of this is to say that what may seem like a contemporary debate, to assign or to not assign homework, is actually a long-simmering issue. For more than one hundred years, homework has been an educational hot potato lobbed between one end of a continuum that sees it as a conduit to more academic rigor, international competitiveness, and mental toughness to the other end that views homework as an unnecessary task negating the importance of free play, ignoring the sanctity of family time, and failing to acknowledge the needs of the whole child. There are compelling, competing, and charismatic points of view on opposite sides of the debate, with parents and educators standing on both sides and everywhere in between.

Homework Viewed from Different Perspectives

No more homework.
No more books.
No more teachers' dirty looks.

These are the opening lines of a little song we used to sing on the school bus at the end of the school year. I'm not proud of that, especially given my current work. The stereotype of teachers assigning homework and children holding negative attitudes about it is a pervasive education cliché that serves as the basis for childhood songs and sitcom humor about schooling. But, what do teachers really think about homework?

Well, the truth may be that most elementary school teachers expend little of their intellectual energy debating whether to assign or to not assign homework. Usually, homework policies are determined on a district-, school-, or grade-level basis, and individual teachers don't have much choice about them. And if there's not a formal homework policy or requirement in place, teachers tend to assign it as a matter of course because generations of teachers before them have done so and because the teachers working in classrooms next door tend to do so. For many, assigning homework is an ingrained professional habit, almost an automatic task. It's what teachers do. Teachers assign homework.

In Section 2, Janine will explain how teacher perceptions, or beliefs about teaching, directly influence their practice and will share research studies on teacher perceptions of homework.

Although assigning homework is almost always an expected part of a teacher's work, the body of research and popular culture references to homework largely ignore the effects on and perceptions of the classroom teachers who assign it, instead focusing mostly on homework's benefits or drawbacks in relation to the impact on the lives of students and their families.

In this section, we'll examine homework from experiences of classroom teachers who assign it.

Teachers' Time Well Spent?

I taught first grade at PS 321, a public school in Brooklyn. Each grade level at our school had its own homework expectations and norms, although I can't recall who determined them. First- through fifth-grade teachers assigned homework from Monday to Thursday nights, so children (and families) had their weekends off. In first grade, we assigned reading time at home, and on most days, a mathematics Homelinks which was created by the publishers of our mathematics curriculum. Beyond that, teachers could assign anything else that corresponded with their studies, inquiries, or other curricular areas.

As a grade, we assigned ten minutes of reading time and ten minutes' worth of other homework in September. This expectation would increase to thirty-five total minutes (twenty minutes of reading and fifteen minutes of other homework) by the end of the year. We used our best guesses to determine the fine line between some homework and too much. In Section 2, Janine shares research on the negative effects of too much homework.

> **There's research on the negative effects of too much homework.**
>
> see Section 2, page 30

Although we had some shared homework norms we followed, teachers at my school were also able to customize homework content to match the schoolwork they were doing in class.

Additionally, the teachers at our school could determine their own homework systems, and there were many! I was one of ten first-grade teachers, and several of us created fresh homework each day that was based on what was going on in class and responsive to children's understandings. This meant that during our lunch period, which was shared with second-grade teachers, there was often a mad dash to the single high-volume copy machine located down on the first floor in our main office where we daily homework makers duplicated our homework assignments.

On most days, I followed a predictable routine. I'd quickly eat my lunch to get to the copy machine, hoping that it wasn't broken or that someone wasn't duplicating hundreds of copies of a whole-school lice alert or some other schoolwide announcement. I had little time to spare, so I always felt relieved (and lucky) when the copy machine was available and working.

Once my homework was duplicated, I'd rush back upstairs to my classroom and use the last moments of my lunch break to load it into my students' homework folders. Later in the day, right before dismissal, I'd take five to fifteen minutes to explain the assignment as quickly as possible to my students and to pass out their homework folders before they packed up to head home for the day.

Several of my colleagues also ran in this race against the clock every day, using our lunch times or our preparation periods in addition to taking time before and after school to handle homework. In fact, some predictable patterns, rhythms, and unspoken courtesies emerged as we tried to accommodate each other's homework needs and systems. Some teachers would use the front end of the lunch period to duplicate their homework, and others (like me) squeezed it in toward the end.

You might wonder why we put ourselves through all of this daily homework hustle and bustle even though this approach to homework often left us harried. There were and are other systems, such as sending home a packet of homework once a week; emailing, posting, or using social media to convey assignments; or having children copy assignments into homework notebooks or daily agendas. Although these systems may alleviate the daily hectic mad-dash feeling I described, it's still the case that any homework system requires that teachers devote at least some of their professional time on the "life cycle of homework."

No matter where in the world I travel to work with teachers, the lack of time to get everything done is the one common, global, across-grade issue that arises. Elementary school teachers everywhere feel pressure to cover more curricula, complete more assessments, gather more data, meet more often with colleagues, and participate on more committees and initiatives, and they devote ever more time to these tasks before, during, and after school. The time management struggle is real, and many teachers find it challenging to prioritize their time when it seems like everything is high priority.

We have to acknowledge that the intellectual work of the homework cycle (planning, creating, explaining, and evaluating homework assignments) and the clerical work of the homework cycle (duplicating, distributing, collecting, and redistributing assignments) demand teachers' precious time and energy.

The time teachers spend on the homework cycle is not available for other essential teaching pursuits, such as short-term planning for the school day, long-term planning for units and projects, creating instructional plans for individuals and small groups, organizing the classroom for teaching and learning, collaborating with colleagues, preparing materials, communicating with families, and so on.

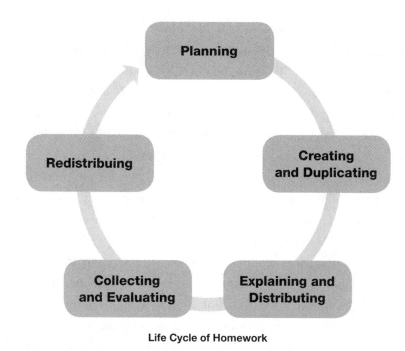

Life Cycle of Homework

Because teachers' time is, indeed, a limited commodity, the decision to use some of it on the homework life cycle suggests that it's essential to create and assign homework that, first and foremost, is worth children's (and teachers') valuable time.

Purposes for Homework

Over the last couple of years, I've asked hundreds of teachers why they assign homework. It seems that that the most typical first responses fall into the following broad categories:

Homework gives children time to *practice* new learning and to *solidify* concepts and understandings.

Homework helps children *develop* organizational skills, time management, and functional work habits.

Homework gives teachers an opportunity to *communicate* with families about school work.

Homework to Practice Skills and Solidify Concepts

During workshops and conferences for teachers, it's common for presenters to reference Malcolm Gladwell's book, *Outliers, The Story of Success*, especially the part about the 10,000 Hour Rule (Gladwell 2008.), which suggests that it takes *a lot* of deliberate practice to master a task or activity. Although the 10,000 Hour Rule was based on limited research and its importance as a factor in education performance is debatable (Macnamara, Hambrick, and Oswald 2014), this information is often used as one of the main rationales for homework assignments—they are intended to give children more time to practice essential skills because school hours just aren't enough.

An implication of the popularity of the 10,000 Hour Rule is that even for schools and individual teachers that consider themselves to be homework minimalists, there are often daily expectations and soft assignments designed to give children more practice with particular tasks. For example, many teachers send home pages of math problems for children to solve, as quickly as possible, to practice their math facts. This sort of homework assignment asks children to practice fast regurgitation of math facts (many of which they may already know), but it may not help their mathematical understanding nor is it likely to encourage a deeply felt love for math. In fact, research suggests that tying math problem-solving and math profiency with speed and timed exercises can increase the likelihood of math anxiety (Boaler 2014).

Most elementary school teachers also assign reading homework each night with the intention of increasing children's reading competence, stamina, and the likelihood they develop a daily reading habit. To this end, reading homework often includes quantity parameters (i.e., "Read for ten minutes" or "Read one chapter"). Sometimes reading homework may task a child with writing-about-reading tasks (i.e., "Write a letter to your character" or "Jot three new vocabulary words from your reading"). Many other children get reading homework that has nothing to do with a book; instead, it's in the form of assigned passages or text excerpts followed by multiple-choice or short-answer questions to practice particular skills for upcoming tests and assessments. These sorts of assignments are often designed with accountability in mind because they can indicate whether or not a child is doing their reading homework each night. In Section 3, we'll share different ways to assign reading at home so that it provides necessary reading practice along with opportunities for children to grow a positive relationship with reading.

Another intention is to provide opportunities for children to practice a skill until they have neared or reached perfection and automaticity with the task. For example, many elementary school teachers assign a variety of practice spelling, handwriting, and keyboarding in the form of drills and exercises with hopes that the extra time spent on these tasks will help children's accuracy as spellers, neatness as writers, and speed as typists. In Section 3, we'll consider alternatives to this kind of homework that features context-free tasks assigned for practice's sake.

Homework as a Scaffold Supporting the Development of Time Management and Organizational Skills

Many elementary school teachers and families view homework as a way of helping children to develop highly functional learning habits, such as the abilities to manage time, organize materials, and remember to carry items back and forth between home and school.

Although teachers can control for the amount of homework they assign and regularly remind families about the expectations regarding time spent on homework tasks (i.e., stop after twenty minutes), it's not always possible to account for how much time individual children spend on their homework, which is often determined by their caregiver. An assignment might take one child fifteen minutes to finish but another child might end up spending an hour on it, even though the teacher's instructions said to spend no more than twenty minutes on the task.

Sometimes, the homework time limits that teachers recommend have unintended consequences. A friend of mine shared the story of her daughter, whose teacher said children should stop working on homework after twenty minutes. Her daughter quickly realized that stopping after twenty minutes might mean temporary relief, but she'd have to finish what was left the next night, along with doing the newly assigned homework. She found herself in homework debt, owing left over and unfinished assignments that had accumulated.

It's difficult to control or manage parental responses to homework. I used to send home a quick "Write a few sentences about something you did over your weekend" kind of assignment each Monday, with clear directions to spend no more than ten minutes on it. Chelsee's mom jotted a note in the margin of Chelsee's half-completed assignment: "Chels is exhausted tonight. We stopped after ten minutes. Hope this is okay!"

On that same assignment, Alex's homework had lots of erasure marks, some that even tore holes through the paper. The spelling and punctuation were conventional and the handwriting neat. A shiny veneer of homework perfection covered the toil and trouble underneath. Alex's homework writing didn't look like anything he had ever written in class, so I asked him how it went. Alex told me it took him all night. "My mom kept making me fix it," he said. Even though I wasn't sure what "all night" meant, I was certain that he spent at least twice as much time as anyone else and was likely under twice as much stress.

I couldn't help but wonder how homework supports elementary-aged children to develop time management and organizational skills, especially when it's typically the adults in the teacher-caregiver-child triad that determine homework quantity and homework time frames as well as the tone and timing for homework completion outside of school. In Section 2, Janine will share research that shows how important adult attitudes are in shaping children's relationships to homework, and then in Section 3, we'll suggest child-centered ways in which children can develop time management and organizational skills.

Homework as a Method of Communication

At most elementary schools, there is usually an evening in the early fall for teachers to share information about the work children will be doing in school for the rest of the year. Whether it's called Curriculum Night or Open House or Meet the Teacher Night, this event provides families a glimpse into the studies, standards, expectations, content, units, and so on that their children will encounter. A common frustration about these events that is shared by teachers and families is that there is never enough time to talk in depth or to ask questions about the year's work. Also, family turnout can be an issue at these events, especially for those with transportation difficulties, conflicting work schedules, overwhelming situations, previous commitments, or even caregiver indifference.

Because there aren't many formalized and efficient opportunities for teachers to discuss curricula with families, homework becomes a curricular messenger, enabling teachers to communicate to families the work their children are doing in school. When parents look at their children's homework, they get a glimpse into what is being taught in the classroom, and if they watch their children do homework or check it after it's done, their children's strengths and struggles with schoolwork may be revealed. Also, the homework folder or notebook itself serves as a carrier pigeon, relaying notes and information back and forth between home and school, even in these days of texts and emails and social media.

Questions for Teachers:

How have you used homework assignments to communicate with families?

What evidence do you have that homework is or is not an effective tool for communication?

Behind-the-Scenes, Off-the-Record Rationales for Homework Assignments

Using homework to provide practice opportunities, to improve time management habits, or to communicate with families are the most common on-the-record responses to the question, "What purpose does homework serve?" These are the expected answers to questions about the purpose of homework because they focus on homework's benefits for children and families. Yet, when teachers and I have the time to talk in more depth about their purposes and intentions that underlie homework, we realize that there are also a few unspoken and off-the-record reasons that many teachers assign homework.

Homework as a Public Relations Tool

When my son Owen entered middle school in fifth grade, he was assigned to a team with Mrs. M. Before the first day of school, Owen complained that he would be soon slammed with homework.

"How do you know this?" we asked.

"Everyone knows it," Owen said. "Mrs. M. gives a ton of homework."

Owen's certainty about his upcoming school year was based solely on the community gossip and student chatter about Mrs. M., a teacher who had a well-known reputation as "the one who assigns tons of homework." The lore about the intensity and quantity of Mrs. M.'s homework had been passed down among kids and parents for years, so when Owen was assigned to Mrs. M.'s team, he braced himself. Some families hope their child will be assigned to her team because of her reputation for the rigor and quantity of homework, but other families worry that their children will be overwhelmed or doubt the necessity of the homework.

During Open School Night in mid-September, even Mrs. M. acknowledged, with good humor, her lingering reputation for giving tons of homework. Although she said that she intentionally reduced the amount she assigned, her reputation as the one who gives tons of homework stubbornly remained.

Homework assignments can be the most public manifestation of what children are doing and learning in their classrooms, and as a result, teachers' reputations are often based on the community's perceptions about their homework.

When parents share their opinions about good teachers versus mediocre teachers, the quantity and quality of homework can be important criteria used to inform their viewpoints. For example, a pair of second-grade twins had two teachers with different homework policies—one teacher assigned quite a bit of daily homework, and the other assigned homework as needed. According to the twins' parents, the teacher who assigned a lot of homework had "very high expectations" of children, and the low-homework teacher was "too easygoing and not challenging enough."

I pay attention to families' chatter about teachers including perceptions of teachers' strength and weaknesses, and I started collecting comments. Here are my interpretations of my very informal "study":

Elementary School Homework Load Assigned	Parents' Perceptions of Teachers	Parents' Perceptions and Feelings Toward Homework Assignments
Consistently moderate to high quantity of homework (i.e., daily for at least thirty minutes, increasing as the child moves through the grades)	Rigorous Strict High expectations of children Hardworking Good teacher	Happy Frustrated Burdensome Appropriate Busywork Helpful Wish there was less homework Wish there was more homework Worry about stressed-out children

(continued)

(continued)

Elementary School Homework Load Assigned	Parents' Perceptions of Teachers	Parents' Perceptions and Feelings Toward Homework Assignments
Consistently low to moderate quantity of homework (possible short daily assignments of reading/math facts practice or days with no homework)	Lazy Loosey-goosey Soft Easygoing Values children's playtime and downtime Disorganized	Happy Frustrated Appropriate Wish there was more homework Wish there was less homework Worry that kids aren't getting enough

Many schools develop standardized homework policies, partly to eliminate inevitable teacher-to-teacher comparisons based on homework, in recognition that quantity and difficulty of homework will be criteria parents use to judge teacher quality. This can be comforting to teachers (and to parents) to know that everyone on a grade gets homework with the same expectations for time and tasks.

In other schools, there may be formal policies or informal agreements that all the teachers on a grade level will send home the exact same assignments to all children in attempts to reduce homework quality comparisons. This approach can be helpful for teachers because then they can share the responsibilities of the homework life cycle. Also, because everyone is sending home the same assignments, the community of parents may be comforted in thinking that all children are getting similar instruction. On the other hand, teachers and parents may find homework uniformity a bit confining because there's no way a universal grade-level homework packet or assignment can perfectly match the work that each class, or an individual child, is doing or has covered on one day or across a particular week.

Homework as a Comfort Object for Grown-Ups

Another off-the-record reason for assigning homework, specifically particular kinds of homework, is that it can provide a measure of security for parents. Teachers often send home assignments largely because they're the kind of work parents expect (or demand) to see their child doing. One third-grade teacher confided that even knowing that lists of spelling words and Friday spelling tests might not be the best way to teach spelling (Palmer and Invernizzi 2014), "I send that kind of work home because parents at my school worry so much about their children's spelling. Spelling lists and spelling tests are familiar to parents and they kind of expect them. I think it makes them feel comfortable when their child has to do things like write words three times, write definitions, or write the words in a sentence. It's what they did when they were in school."

This sort of comfort homework designed to assuage parents' worries may also include tasks such as handwriting practice, either manuscript or cursive, because many parents worry about their children's handwriting and, again, they remember handwriting practice from their own education.

Teachers also use homework to assign practice with math facts in the form of drills and worksheets, especially as a counterbalance in schools and districts in which the approach to math instruction may not emphasize rote memorization of math facts. When parents worry that their children might be falling behind, teachers often tailor homework to calm their fears and to accommodate their concerns.

Homework as a Curricular Overflow Container

Time is always an issue for classroom teachers, and it's hard to cover everything within a school day and across the year. Teachers have to constantly prioritize how they spend their instructional time, and usually, the priorities become the curricular areas or tasks that are tested, counted, quantified, or mandated.

That leaves a lot of pieces of curriculum that may not be urgent priorities, data-wise, but still need to be covered, somewhere and somehow. These items are often housed in homework assignments. Based on conversations with many teachers, here are the kinds of tasks and content included on homework simply because there may not be time to work on these things in school:

Can homework be more than this? Yes. You'll find a great variety of examples in Section 3.

- keyboarding
- cursive and manuscript handwriting practice
- science work and investigations
- social studies work and investigations
- "finish" work (i.e., adding illustrations to writing pieces; art projects; worksheet packets, workbook pages; and so on)

Homework: Families and Educators Share Similar Homework Benefits and Frustrations

Attitudes and beliefs about homework can wax and wane for teachers and families. Sometimes they may feel so certain that homework is a good practice for all involved, yet at other times homework just might seem like another educational hoop that everyone is jumping through.

Some families may need and appreciate the extra guiding nudge that teacher-assigned homework can provide. After all, it might be grounds for a battle when parents of a reluctant reader demand that their child read at home, but it can be very helpful if the teacher also makes the request through a homework assignment. Homework may provide an opportunity in which teachers and families can provide backup for each other as they share the goal of helping their children get stronger in particular skills or curricula areas.

The Difficulty of Differentiation

Many people consider the ability to differentiate instruction and experiences in the classroom an important characteristic of the best teachers. Teachers attend workshops and conferences, acquire degrees and certificates, and read professional literature and pertinent research in their efforts to learn how to differentiate instruction to meet children where they are as learners and human beings. It may make sense, then, to extend the disposition toward differentiation to homework, to accommodate the incredible variety of student personalities, home situations, struggles, strengths, quirks, and dispositions.

Yet, when it comes to differentiating homework, it may very well be the case that teachers' energy, efforts, and sense of urgency for differentiation are depleted during the school day. Teachers usually assign their whole class the same homework, even though they know it will be easy-breezy for some children and incredibly difficult for others, both in terms of the children's abilities to handle homework content, the children's dispositions to self-motivate, and the families' styles and abilities to offer support.

When asked about homework differentiation, a fourth-grade teacher said, "As I'm making my homework, I know who will likely struggle, and I can picture who will finish it in ten minutes. But I just can't create twenty-four different assignments. I differentiate for my kids all day, and I just can't pull it together to differentiate this every day, too." He went on to say that he has often created and assigned a couple of different levels of homework—a harder homework packet and easier one, depending on each child's needs and strengths. "In my experience, when I send home 'leveled' packets, it has stressed out kids or their parents, especially if they know they got the 'easier' one. I usually get a couple of notes or calls from parents when I do this."

This brings us to the issue of parents' and caregivers' relationships to their children's homework, both in terms of their attitudes about it and their interactions with it. Some parents might value homework and view its completion as a worthy way for their child to spend time, whereas other parents might hold negative attitudes about homework, resenting the time it takes away from their child's other pursuits or because they struggle to see the value of the assignments. In Section 2, Janine will share research about the importance and effect of parental attitudes toward school work.

Many teachers and students describe conditions at home that reveal a vast continuum of support. Some families may not offer any help or guidance with homework, due to their situational circumstances (caregivers who have to work and/or deal with family distractions and struggles; children with extremely busy after-school lives), accessibility limitations (caregivers who may have limited language proficiency, content knowledge, and/or technology resources), or their general attitudes about homework (caregivers who believe that homework is their children's responsibility; caregivers who prioritize other aspects of their child's lives; caregivers who don't value homework).

At the opposite end of the continuum, there are caregivers who offer support in a variety of ways, such as supervising (naming the time and place of homework), helicoptering (staying close by to make sure the child is doing it and doing it well), conferring (offering support or strategy guidance with challenges), or taking over the homework altogether (doing it for the child or redoing it if it doesn't meet the parents' standards).

Even though some teachers or district policies might make recommendations for how parents can best support their children as they do homework, parents and caregivers may have family norms and personal expectations for how the work will go. Many parents and families have time conflicts and financial limitations around the supports and enrichments they can provide. For these reasons, teachers know that giving the same assignment to their students is certainly not a guarantee that each child will experience it in the same way.

In Section 2, Janine will share research that suggests ways that caregivers can provide a positive environment as well as support and encouragement around their children's school work.

The Dearth of Meaningful Feedback

Stickers. Smiley Faces. "Good."
Check Plus. Check. Check Minus.
Circled Problems.
"See Me!"

This isn't a bad version of a homework haiku. It's Jeopardy! If those items were the answers found in a square under the category "School Matters," the question could be,

What is the typical kind of feedback
teachers provide on elementary school
students' homework?

Along the life cycle of homework, there is a point when the teacher looks at the homework to evaluate it or to provide feedback, yet children most often receive the kind of feedback that simply lets them know their teacher checked their work and acknowledged its completion. As I recall my own practices with homework evaluation, I confess that I often outsourced that part of the homework cycle to either the classroom learning aide (paraprofessional) or to my student-teacher. They, too, used my method of feedback, the smiley face drawn in brightly colored Crayola markers. At best, we would make vague, bland, and usually flattering comments in the margins of homework, along the lines of: "Neat work!" or "Good job!" Even in the moment, I recognized that not giving meaningful feedback was a lost learning opportunity, yet I did not know where to find the time to connect with children about their homework.

Research by John Hattie (2012) indicates the importance and power of meaningful feedback. At its best, meaningful feedback provides yet another learning opportunity for children. Yet in most cases, because of time constraints and competing priorities, teachers can only manage to give homework a cursory glance and a quick mark of acknowledgement. It seems that parents and teachers both have low expectations for homework feedback. Yet, without meaningful feedback, what does the child learn from the work and what does the teacher learn about the child?

It's probably impossible to make everyone happy about homework. For most parents, there seems to be a "Goldilocks effect" at work—with regard to quality, they tend to find their children's homework too hard, too easy, or just right, and with regard to quantity, there is too much, too little, or just enough. For most teachers, there is an "inevitability effect." Generations of teachers before us have assigned homework, so it's almost an automated practice. Homework policies are handed down from year to year and passed around from class to class, and many teachers, myself included, assign it whether or not they view it as an effective learning opportunity for their students and without regard to what research might say about the practice.

In Section 2, Janine will share the latest research on homework, especially about the ways it can support children's learning habits and dispositions as well as roles that caregivers can assume that provide support and encouragement. In Section 3, I'll return to suggest ideas for how to use the research to share a more expansive vision of homework policies and assignments that can help all teachers support all of their students' engagement and investment in their own learning.

WHY NOT? WHAT WORKS?

Homework That Promotes Lifelong Learning Behaviors

JANINE BEMPECHAT

As a developmental psychologist who studies achievement motivation in children and adolescents, I am deeply engaged in research on the benefits and drawbacks of homework. Homework as commonly understood is a task or tasks teachers assign students to complete during noninstructional time (e.g., after school, during study periods [Cooper, Robinson, and Patall 2006]). Beyond that common definition, what teachers actually assign for homework varies greatly. Kathy and I want readers to leave this book with a more expansive and positive sense of what homework can be. More than just "getting it done," homework can be an opportunity to foster positive beliefs about learning, establish meaningful habits of mind, and forge an academic identity. In this section, I share what researchers have learned about the relationship between homework, achievement, and motivation and research-based principles on how teachers and parents can support children in their homework experiences. I close with an analysis of the national discourse on homework in which I argue that high-quality, developmentally appropriate homework plays a critical role in socializing children into their roles as emerging students and young scholars.

The Ebb and Flow of Homework Practices Over Time

> From September 5 to June 1 we cease to operate as a family and become "teachers" from 4 until 11 o'clock P.M. We can't go anywhere or do anything, even on weekends. Our patience wears thin, tempers flare, and worst of all, the children, all four of them, are getting to like school less and less.

For a great many parents today, the above quotation jibes with their family's experiences, especially during the later school years. It may surprise you to learn that this quote appeared in an article over fifty years ago, one arguing that homework should be abolished (Jones and Ross 1964). Concern over homework dates back over a hundred years and has tended to ebb and flow along with emerging views about healthful activities for young children and prevailing public policy regarding the ability of American students to compete with their international peers (Gill and Schlossman 2003). Much has been written about the ways in which the launch of Sputnik in 1957 prompted educators and parents to reexamine and strengthen homework policies in public schools (Gill and Schlossman 2004). Similar concerns about and commitment to homework have been present since the 1980s, when international comparisons of academic achievement began showing American students to be seriously lacking relative to their Asian, Canadian, and European counterparts (Beaton et al. 1996; Stevenson, Chen, and Lee 1993).

Along with concerns over the relative competitiveness of American students on the global stage, we have seen increasing reports in the media of overwhelmed students and understandably distraught parents. An unreasonably demanding homework load is likely to affect students' mental health, undermine learning, and interfere with family time. Negative effects of homework so challenge its value that some communities in the United States have limited assigned homework or eliminated it altogether, especially in elementary school. Is that a fair response? To answer this question, let's first consider current trends in homework quantity—not just what teachers assign, but also how much time students describe spending on homework.

How Much Homework Do U.S. Students Do?

In contrast to the general perception, it appears that, on average, American students do not do that much homework. For example, in a 2007 survey ninth to twelfth graders reported doing an average of 6.8 hours of homework per week. Less than half of these students (42 percent) reported doing homework five days per week (National Center for Education Statistics, or NCES, 2011). A recent survey found that among nine-, thirteen-, and seventeen-year-olds, the most commonly reported amount of time spent on homework the previous day was less than one hour, and the percentage of students who reported having done more than two hours was minimal, even at the high school level (5 percent, 7 percent, and 13 percent among nine-, thirteen-, and seventeen-year-olds, respectively (National Assessment of Educational Progress, or NAEP, 2013). Regrettably, we cannot know from these data what "less than one hour" means. We gain a better sense of homework assigned and completed from a recent NCES study that surveyed teacher expectations and parents' reports of reading and math homework among the same cohort of children as they progressed from first to third to fifth grade (Warkentien et al. 2008). Teachers expected and parents reported more homework completed on a typical evening as children got older. More

As Kathy explained in Section 1, families sometimes make judgments about teacher quality based on volume of homework alone. Later in this section, Janine will share a different model of family communication, the TIPS program, and Kathy will offer some ways teachers can better communicate with families through homework in Section 3.

specifically, the percentage of first, third, and fifth graders whose teachers expected them to spend thirty minutes on reading/language arts homework on a typical evening increased from 17 percent (first grade) to 24 percent (third grade) and finally to 38 percent (fifth grade). Parents' reports mirrored these expectations, in that the percentage of students whose parents reported that they completed homework five or more times a week increased from 38 percent in first grade to 47 percent in third grade to 51 percent in fifth grade.

It is interesting to note that in a widely cited representative survey of parents' attitudes about homework, findings showed that a majority of parents (60 percent at the elementary level and 58 percent at the secondary level) believe that their children are assigned the "right amount" of homework (MetLife 2007). At both school levels, more parents believe that children receive too little rather than too much homework (26 percent too little as compared to 12 percent too much at the elementary level, and 23 percent too little versus 19 percent too much at the secondary level). Of course, how much time students spend on homework does not give us information on the quality of the task. Furthermore, average time on homework is just that—an average. Of course, some students may take more or less time to complete a given task than others. Still, in terms of measurement of time, studies suggest that, on average, students are not burdened by excess homework.

What Are the Benefits of Homework?

With the focus in today's schools on making research-based decisions, it is a challenge to have definite answers regarding the benefits of homework given that most of the evidence is correlational. Available experimental research studies, small in number, have shown that students who are randomly assigned homework show measureable improvements in academic achievement as compared to students who are not assigned homework (Cooper, Robinson, and Patall 2006). As Cooper and his colleagues have noted, these findings suggest a causal relationship, but are limited in scope.

Most research on the relationship between homework and academic achievement is correlational because of obvious difficulties carrying out a randomization protocol for homework assignments, either between students within a classroom or between classrooms in the same school. Of course, correlation does not imply causality. But at the high school level especially, a large body of correlational research has consistently shown statistically significant findings for the association between homework completion and school achievement (Cooper, Robinson, and Patall 2006; Trautwein et al. 2009). These findings, coupled with the paucity of studies showing the opposite correlation, makes the relationship between these variables difficult to dismiss as spurious.

At the elementary school level, research findings are somewhat mixed. At best, the relationship between homework and academic achievement in elementary grades is weak. A positive relationship between homework completed and school grades has been reported among second and fourth graders (Cooper et al. 1998) and fourth through sixth graders (Valle et al. 2016). Yet another study reported a negative association between homework and achievement in elementary school (Cooper 1989). Still other studies have reported no relationship between homework completed and grades or achievement test scores (Cooper, Robinson, and Patall 2006).

It is important to note, however, that most research examines homework in general, not subject-specific homework. With this limitation in mind, a recent meta-analysis focused on the the relationship between homework in math-science and academic achievement (Fan et al. in press). Results showed a stronger relationship between math-science homework and achievement among elementary students compared to middle school students, contradicting previous findings (e.g., Cooper et al. 2006) and suggesting that more clarity on the homework-achievement relationship may result from subject-specific studies. With respect to math, these researchers proposed that the stronger homework-achievement relationship among elementary school students might result from the fact that teachers tend to assign more homework in math than in other subjects, and that in elementary school in particular, math homework is typically more frequently assigned and shorter in nature. Previous research has suggested that these two characteristics may be more useful in fostering achievement in younger students than assignments that are longer and less frequently assigned (Cooper 1989; Fan et al. in press). Finally, Fan and colleagues note that the positive homework-achievement relationship may also be due to parents being more involved in helping their children with math homework in elementary than middle school and more skilled in elementary than middle school level mathematics.

Separate from the issue of subject-specific research, it may be that differentiation in the type of homework that is given at the younger grade levels from the homework assigned in older grades is also needed. Researchers have suggested that developmental issues, including the ability to focus (Muhlenbruck et al. 2000) and the efficiency of young children's study skills (Dufresne and Kobasigawa 1998), may impact the effectiveness of homework on academic achievement in the early grades. Although research does not point to a definitive relationship between homework and academic achievement at the elementary level, by not assigning homework we may be missing an opportunity to develop habits and identity that promote long-term academic achievement. The field would benefit from more systematic studies that examine the impact of specific types of homework that are developmentally appropriate with younger students.

In Section 3, Kathy offers examples of homework practices that focus on younger students.

The Power of Adaptive Learning Beliefs

Children's learning beliefs and behaviors have a critical effect on how they approach school assignments (Dweck and Molden 2005). Of course, children's learning beliefs develop within family and school contexts and are profoundly influenced by parents and teachers (Pomerantz, Grolnick, and Price 2005; Rosenthal 2002). A positive orientation toward learning is far more favorable than a negative approach, in part because it helps children remain resilient when they encounter challenges in their schoolwork. For example, children who believe that failure is the result of lack of effort (a quality we tend to perceive as internal and controllable) are much more likely to invest more effort in their learning than those who believe failure to be the result of lack of ability (a quality we tend to believe is internal but uncontrollable; Weiner 2005). A variety of studies have demonstrated that teachers and parents can foster positive approaches to learning through the routine of homework, and I discuss this research later.

> When all homework is assigned, children can miss out on opportunities to foster these adaptive learning beliefs. Kathy will share homework options based on choice in Section 3.

Self-Regulation

Self-regulation, which develops over time, is a critical aspect of the motivation to achieve. In effective self-regulation, students monitor their performance and adjust their strategies as a result of feedback (metacognitive awareness); assess their interests, perceptions of ability, and autonomy while they work on a task (motivational awareness); and put in place optimal conditions (such as a favored location) that maximize their particular learning preferences (behavioral awareness) (Zimmerman and Schunk 2011). There is no doubt that as children get older, the tasks teachers require of them become more demanding and require more time to complete. Of necessity, all children increasingly need to develop self-regulatory strategies (e.g., planning and time management) to direct their learning and succeed in school. This is one of several reasons (including helping students prepare for upcoming lessons, encouraging peer interaction through collaborative assignments, and enhancing the connection between home and school) that elementary school teachers endorse homework (Epstein and Van Voorhis 2001). Indeed, a significant majority of elementary (88 percent) and secondary (95 percent) school teachers believe that homework helps students learn more and agree that the practice develops sense of responsibility (98 percent of elementary and 97 percent of secondary school teachers) (MetLife 2007). Although research on the relationship between teachers' homework beliefs and students' achievement may be limited, it is imperative that we value teachers' voice and experience. Indeed, there is significant literature that demonstrates that teachers' beliefs and perceptions are the strongest predictors of their pedagogical practices (Biesta, Priestley, and Robinson 2015; Jimenez-Silva and Olson 2012). One question that Kathy will address in Section 3 is how teachers can do more than expect these behaviors by teaching and nurturing them through specific kinds of homework.

Most teachers' primary focus in designing homework for young children is not achievement per se, but rather self-regulation (Cooper et al. 2001). Many teachers view homework as important for the development of positive learning orientations and behaviors, including responsibility, perseverance, and managing distractions (Cooper and Valentine 2001; Coutts 2004; Epstein and Van Voorhis 2001). In a study probing the effect of homework on academic achievement in elementary versus secondary school, researchers examined teachers' perceptions of the extent to which they believed that homework helps students learn, fosters study skills, and encourages time management skills (Muhlenbruck et al. 2000). Results showed that teachers of different grade levels viewed homework's utility differently. Although all teachers reported assigning homework for these three reasons, compared with high school teachers, elementary school teachers perceived homework to be significantly more useful for fostering time management. This suggests that in elementary school teachers use homework not only for developing content knowledge, but, more purposefully, to foster time management, a critical component of self-regulation. Indeed, elementary school teachers are more likely than their secondary school peers to report making frequent use of homework to foster study skills (MetLife 2007).

As Harris Cooper and his colleagues (1998) have noted, the value of homework in the early grades may not be realized until children are older. Their research supports the assignment of homework in early grades, not necessarily because of any proximal impact on achievement, but rather because of its potential to have a long-term impact. We cannot predict that moment when children will internalize behaviors. The acquisition of any learning is complex and occurs over time. This presents an argument for providing children with repeated opportunities, through homework, to develop critical study skills. In other words, effective study skills and time management strategies, scaffolded by elementary school teachers through the use of homework, are likely to result in higher achievement as children get older. Other research supports this conclusion: homework has been found to foster positive learning beliefs and self-regulatory behavior, such as planning and self-monitoring (Bembenutty and Zimmerman 2003). These positive approaches to learning are in turn associated with higher academic achievement, more homework completion, higher perceived self-efficacy, and greater personal responsibility for learning from elementary through secondary school (Ramdass and Zimmerman 2011; Xu and Wu 2013).

Given that homework may indeed assist in developing the foundation for adaptive learning beliefs and behaviors, how much homework is appropriate for children at different ages? Harris Cooper has proposed the "ten-minute rule" (e.g., twenty minutes in second grade, forty minutes in fourth grade), which is endorsed by the National Parent Teacher Association and the National Education Association (Cooper 1989). Depending on the school, this guideline may or may not include reading, which most teachers believe should become part of every child's after-school routine. At the high school level, many school districts recommend about thirty minutes per subject, with more homework as needed in Honors or Advanced Placement (AP) classes. There does indeed appear to be a point of diminishing returns where amounts of homework are concerned. At the middle school level, the positive relationship between homework and achievement peaks at about ninety minutes per day. In high school, optimal achievement gains occur between ninety minutes and two and a half hours in total daily (Cooper, Robinson, and Patall 2006). Despite these findings, we know that some teachers—especially those in more affluent communities—assign much more than this (Galloway, Conner, and Pope 2013). We also know that students who cut into their sleep time to get their homework done (a phenomenon most present at the high school level) undermine their learning and comprehension (Gillen-O'Neel, Huynh, and Fuligni 2013). This leads us to wonder whether the pressure to cover a great amount of material (for example, in preparation for AP exams) may lead teachers to expect students to cover new content through homework. This is a question worthy of future research.

> **Too much homework doesn't help children. Janine encourages teachers and families to be mindful of how much time children are spending on homework.**

Families Matter!

Learning beliefs and behaviors conducive to academic achievement do not develop in a vacuum. Rather, they are fostered at an early age—when parents have more sway in encouraging children to adopt responsible homework and study habits (Xu and Corno 1998)—and encouraged over time through supportive scaffolding from parents and teachers. Although there are exceptions, most parents wish to be involved in their children's learning and believe that their involvement is an important aspect of their role as parents (Hoover-Dempsey et al. 2001). As I will explain later, homework gives parents a variety of ways to help their children assume the role of mature learner. Many parents also believe that success in doing homework leads to success in school and accept that even if homework is a struggle for their children at times, it is necessary to enhance learning (Hoover-Dempsey, Bassler, and Burrow 1995). In addition, parents agree that teachers expect them to be involved in their children's learning, and they want information and support from their children's teachers that will help them support their children (Walker et al. 2009).

Teachers, in turn, welcome parents' involvement because it indicates support, strengthens the connection between home and school, and fosters higher achievement. Although there exists debate over assigning homework in early elementary school, surveys have shown that parents are supportive of homework because they believe that it fosters essential strengths of character, such as personal responsibility, and helps children learn more in school, a belief held by 89 percent of parents of elementary school children (MetLife 2007). As I show below, parents' perceptions about the value of homework are nontrivial—they predict the ways in which they interact with their children around their homework tasks, which, in turn, predict students' academic achievement (see, for example, Dumont et al. 2014). Furthermore, high school students tend to agree with parents and teachers that homework is important, reinforces learning, and fosters achievement (Coutts 2004; Fairbanks, Clark, and Barry 2005).

For all socioeconomic groups, parental involvement in children's schooling in general is widely seen as beneficial for children's outcomes (see Bempechat and Shernoff 2012 for a review). The positive outcomes associated with parent involvement include higher grade point average and achievement test scores, greater rates of high school completion, improved school attendance, more positive attitudes about school, and greater socioemotional well-being (Comer 2005; Eccles and Gootman 2002; Mapp et al. 2008; Pomerantz, Moorman, and Litwack 2007). As important and less discussed, extended family members wish to do their part in helping children with homework assignments and projects (Li et al. 2008). This is definitely the case for the more than 2.7 million grandparent caregivers who have primary responsibility for raising their grandchildren (Ellis and Simmons 2014). Given that the bulk of research is conducted with parents, I refer to "parent" involvement here but emphasize that many children are supported by aunts, uncles, older siblings and cousins, and of course, grandparents.

In ideal circumstances, research suggests that teachers also appreciate hearing directly from parents when homework is experienced as overly demanding and welcome opportunities to work in concert with parents to develop homework strategies that are sensitive to individual students' learning needs (Gilliland 2007). Of course, context matters, and ideal circumstances may not always be present. Aware of the positive impact of parent involvement, teachers are eager for parents—especially those with low incomes—to be involved in and connected to their children's learning (Epstein and Van Voorhis 2001). Teachers can marshal two noteworthy research findings to support parents who may be uncertain how to provide their children with truly useful homework help and advice, and I provide examples below. First, there are many ways in which parents can interact with their children in connection with schoolwork to foster achievement (Patall, Cooper, and Robinson 2008). Second, parents' own attitudes about and behavior related to homework have a profound influence on children's own developing attitudes and behavior (Pomerantz, Ng, and Wang 2006). These research findings apply equally to parents across the socioeconomic spectrum.

Meaningful parent involvement goes beyond helping with homework; it is multifaceted and multidimensional. Parents may be involved behaviorally (by attending back-to-school night), personally (by inquiring about and expressing interest in children's daily school experiences), and cognitively (by providing homework help or exposing children to intellectually enriching activities, such as going to the library) (Grolnick and Slowiaczek 1994). Perhaps without realizing it, parents undertake a variety of actions that support the development of skills related to self-regulation, including helping their children establish homework routines, providing a dedicated space for schoolwork, helping children manage their time, and recognizing the conditions at home that help or hinder their ability to get their homework done (Cooper, Lindsey, and Nye 2000).

Scaffolding Self-Regulation

An observational study of third graders and their parents found that parents tried to arrange things in the home to minimize distractions and keep their children's attention and motivation on task. Over time, children integrated the self-regulation strategies modeled by their parents into their homework practices. "Everyday experiences with homework provide clear opportunities for children to learn to cope with various difficulties and distractions associated with doing homework" (Xu and Corno 1998, 430). Setting rules is particularly influential. Parents should convey their expectations by establishing clear parameters about when and where homework is to be done and positively reinforce their children's compliance. This encourages children to internalize their parents' rules and develop helpful self-regulation strategies (Patall, Cooper, and Robinson 2008). Parents communicate subtle messages about their children's education. For example, an immigrant parent might explain that the difficulties of immigration have been made worthwhile because of the educational opportunities now afforded to their children. These messages can positively influence children's academic achievement, even if parents rarely help with homework, interact with their children's teachers, or attend school-related events (Jeynes 2010; Li et al. 2008).

Modeling a Positive Attitude About Homework

Parents' attitudes about homework profoundly influence their children's achievement beliefs and outcomes (Cooper et al. 1998; Else-Quest, Hyde, and Hejmadi 2008; Hong, Milgram, and Rowell 2004; Hoover-Dempsey et al. 2001; Pomerantz, Ng, and Wang 2006). Children's natural attitude toward homework tends to be negative (Shernoff and Vandell 2007), but despite the stress occasionally experienced by children and their parents, there is much that teachers can do to help parents foster strategies that will enhance their children's homework experiences and academic achievement. Importantly, the ways in which parents offer assistance matters. Unsolicited assistance promotes parent-child conflict and negatively affects academic self-concept, homework self-sufficiency, and homework persistence (Dumont et al. 2012; Silinskas et al. 2013). Being overly controlling or limiting involvement to monitoring also negatively affects achievement (Pomerantz, Moorman, and Litwack 2007; Silinskas et al. 2015). A positive attitude and positive emotions (interest, humor, and pride, for example) are more predictive of higher achievement than expressions of negative emotions and parent-child tension (Else-Quest, Hyde, and Hejmadi 2008). Teachers can underscore for all parents, regardless of income, that they are uniquely positioned to create a supportive atmosphere that allows children to experience greater enjoyment, intrinsic interest, higher self-perceptions of competence, and higher achievement (Xu and Corno 2003).

> Ideally, homework experiences can be positive enough so that the momentum for families' positive attitude is entirely authentic. You'll see a wide variety of those kinds of experiences in Section 3.

Concerns have been appropriately raised about lower-income families who, compared with more affluent families, are unlikely to have the social and material resources readily available to support their children's homework completion. Homework can become yet another stress for families facing the pressures of poverty. Carefully designed parent coaching programs, such as the TIPS (Teachers Involve Parents in Schoolwork) program I describe later, have been successful in empowering lower-income parents to enhance their children's homework experiences, especially in elementary school. Individual meetings, workshops, and regular phone calls prompt these parents to see to it that their children complete homework and experience less frustration and fewer problems (such as forgetting it at school) (see Patall, Cooper, and Robinson 2008 for a review).

One study of elementary school teachers in an urban area found that most did not assign homework that could only be completed using a computer. The teacher, the school, or the community provided materials—crayons, paper, dictionaries—students needed to complete their homework. Many of these teachers established homework clubs that met before or after school or made themselves available before or after school. Two thirds did not assign homework that required the help of an adult, and all helped students strategize how to get homework assistance, including reaching out to siblings and extended family members, working with a homework buddy, and joining a homework club (Brock et al. 2007). Of course, such sensitivity to families' needs does not preclude family involvement. As I discussed above, family involvement takes many forms beyond actual help with homework and is important and meaningful in communicating families' commitment to children's schooling. Some opponents of homework argue that there are other compelling ways in which children can learn responsibility and self-regulation. To the extent that this is true, it does not negate the value of homework. There is no reason that homework cannot become an integral part of "family time." The noteworthy TIPS model is an especially illustrative example of homework as family time.

TIPS is a teacher-designed interactive program developed by Johns Hopkins sociologist Joyce Epstein to draw low-income parents into children's daily school experiences through homework. Typically, teachers assign tasks that have clearly defined roles for students and their family members. For example, students may be given a prompt to write a story, then read it to and ask questions about it of a family member. The family member then gives teachers feedback on whether the child understood the activity and could discuss it, and the extent to which he or she and the child enjoyed the activity. In all subject areas, the TIPS model fostered greater homework completion, more family involvement, and more positive attitudes about homework compared with classrooms in which TIPS was not implemented (Epstein 1995). TIPS-involved students were more likely to believe that family members enjoyed working with them on their assignments, helped them understand what they were learning, and enjoyed hearing about what they were learning; they also believed they could talk with family members about the topic in question (Van Voorhis 2011). Studies of the academic impact of TIPS in sixth and eighth grades show that it boosts achievement in writing, mathematics, and science. A longitudinal study of TIPS mathematics homework compared the mathematics achievement and attitudes of third and fourth graders, as well as the attitudes of their parents, in classrooms where TIPS was and was not implemented. In TIPS classrooms, students performed better on standardized tests, and they and their parents developed more positive beliefs and attitudes about learning mathematics (Van Voorhis 2011).

The TIPS model of parent involvement promotes effective homework. Assignments are collaboratively designed and teachers purposefully involve students' families. A letter home, which students sign and date, explains the purpose of the assignment in one sentence. For example, math assignments contain four elements:

1. "Look this over" describes a math skill as taught in class. Students explain to a family member how the skill was taught, and the answer is supplied.
2. In "Now try this," students apply that knowledge to a similar problem, explaining to family members how they are solving the problem. (The solution is provided on the flip side of the page.)

3. "Practice and more practice" sets out a series of related problems. Students ask family members for help when they need it
   or explain how they arrived at the correct solution.
4. "In the real world" encourages interactions. Students and family members discuss how the particular math skill is applied at
   home or in similar situations.

When the assignment is completed, family members indicate whether
or not the child needs more help with this task, reflect on the assignment, and sign the homework sheet (Epstein and Van Voorhis 2001).
Assignments like this are clear, involve academic skill building in an efficient manner, and instill ownership and competence in an engaging way.

The cost of implementing high-quality parent coaching programs
has prompted low-cost but effective alternatives. In a recent study
(Bergman 2015), randomly chosen low-income parents of high school
students received detailed updates about their children's missing assignments (the treatment group). Close to 79 percent received this information through text messages; the remainder preferred email alerts or
phone calls. Messages were sent several times a month over a six-month
period, and course grades were sent every five to eight weeks. Changes
in parent involvement were then compared with that of parents who did
not receive these messages (the control group). Parents in the treatment
group lowered their estimate of the degree of effort they believed their
children invested in school. The negative information they received
about their children's missing homework assignments and performance
led them to increase their participation in parent-child conferences, and
they were significantly more likely to contact the school. Parents in the
treatment group monitored their children's progress more closely, took
away privileges, and talked more about college, even though they were
minimally involved in helping their children with schoolwork. In short,
parents' increased monitoring and involvement served as educational
messages that conveyed their expectation that their children invest
more effort in their schoolwork.

This intervention also had a positive impact on student effort and achievement. Teachers noted improved student work habits, a significant decrease in skipping class and failing to complete assignments, and a significant increase in attending tutoring sessions. Students reported that they were much less likely to do their homework at the last minute. Their math grades and grade point average increased significantly, and these increases continued into the next year, when the protocol was no longer in place. These positive outcomes came at a minimal investment of both time and money, and perhaps aspects of this program could be implemented at the elementary school level.

Teachers' Critical Role in the Homework Process

Like parents, teachers believe homework fosters personal responsibility as well as academic achievement; many also believe it gives students opportunities to review material and practice skills and reinforces what has been taught in school (Brock et al. 2007; Xu and Corno 1998). Of course, teachers view homework as useful feedback on how well students understand material at a particular point in time (Xu and Yuan 2003). Nor is there any doubt that it plays a critical role in fostering self-regulation and academic self-efficacy. Research in elementary school through college supports homework as being a key vehicle through which positive learning beliefs and behavior can be developed and strengthened (Bembenutty 2009; Ramdass and Zimmerman 2011; Schmitz and Perels 2011). In one study, a number of fourth-grade teachers attended a three-day seminar on how to encourage time management skills in their students. Then, over a five-week period, they taught their students to employ a variety of self-regulatory strategies for managing their homework, including setting goals, self-evaluating, self-monitoring, and planning. Compared with students who did not receive this training, those who did demonstrated improved time management and self-reflection, as well as increased self-efficacy, effort, interest, and a desire for mastery; they also showed a decrease in helplessness (Stoeger and Ziegler 2008). More recently, researchers assigned students in one of two seventh-grade classrooms (the experimental group) to receive math homework that included metacognitive prompts (Özcan and Erktin 2015). Prior to beginning their homework assignments, students in the experimental group were asked to reflect on the previous week's lessons (what they learned, what was easy/hard) and to indicate when they would start their homework assignments and what they thought

> There are so many positive opportunities in homework for children to learn these essential adaptive learning beliefs that the focus needs to be not on whether to assign homework, but how to assign homework in meaningful ways.

might be difficult about the tasks in question. Upon completion, these students were asked to record when and how long it took them to complete the assignments, to judge the assignments' difficulty level, and to note which problems they were and were not able to solve. The students in the second classroom (the control group) received the same homework assignments, but without the metacognitive prompts. Prior to this intervention, math scores between the two groups were not significantly different. After the intervention, results showed that relative to students in the control group, those in the experimental group attained significantly higher math grades. The authors note that this metacognitive enhancement posed no additional work for teachers and did not impinge on classroom instruction time.

The standards teachers set for homework completion also influence the amount of time students, especially lower achievers, invest in it: less conscientious students invest more effort in their homework when they know their teachers check its completion (Trautwein and Ludtke 2007; Watkins and Stevens 2013). Similarly, students are more likely to adopt homework management strategies when they know teachers will be grading and discussing their homework assignments (Núñez et al. 2015; Xu and Wu 2013).

But homework can also trigger negative attitudes, especially when students see their homework load as too high (Cooper, Robinson, and Patall 2006). What, then, constitutes helpful homework?

Competence Through Focused Tasks and Timely Feedback

Homework should have a *clear purpose* that is communicated through a method that fosters understanding and meaning. For example, rather than assigning the all-too-familiar task of writing definitions of ten words, teachers can engage students in vocabulary building by having them chart or map relational sets of words (Cobb and Blachowicz 2016). Such an assignment can provide important feedback on what students know and understand (or do not know and understand) (Vatterott 2010).

Homework should focus on *skill building*. At the upper grades, cooperative learning through group assignments, when carefully designed and monitored, can be more effective than assignments completed individually (Cooper 2007). Homework should also instill *competence*. This doesn't mean it should be easy—quite the contrary. But researchers and educators agree that material not covered in the classroom should not be assigned as homework (Darling-Hammond and Ifill-Lynch 2006; Protheroe 2009). Further, one-size-fits-all homework denies the importance of differentiated instruction, a key factor in enhancing reading instruction in the early grades (Bigelman and Peterson 2016). Indeed, homework assignments should be individualized and differentiated so that struggling students will be successful (Cooper 2007). Vatterott (2010) distinguishes between task-based and time-based homework and suggests that the latter is a nontaxing way for teachers to conceptualize and enact differentiated homework. Rather than having students complete all questions on a given task, students can be instructed to respond to as many questions as they can in twenty minutes (students who wish to can of course work longer). Careful scaffolding fosters self-perceptions of competence, so clear instructions are critical. Instead of just asking students to read a chapter, teachers can have them note the ideas that stand out and record questions they have.

In mathematics homework, content and the balance of easier and harder questions matter. Studies have compared the effectiveness of homework that covers what was taught that day, includes practice related to previously taught topics, or introduces preparatory content material for a future topic. Distributed practice, a homework strategy in which assignments include items learned previously along with preparatory content material for future learning, is more effective in fostering learning than homework that is focused on same-day content only (Cooper 2008). Homework that intersperses easy and hard items fosters greater accuracy and completion and is seen as less difficult, less laborious, and taking less time than homework that does not (see Cooper 2007 for a more detailed review). In addition, math homework that requires students to transfer what they have learned to new problems (extension homework) promotes greater learning than homework that provides students with opportunities to review what they have learned (practice homework) or that asks students to read about a topic that is to be discussed in a subsequent class (preparation homework) (Rosário et al. 2015).

> **Homework that balances what children learned that day with future learning reinforces the forward momentum of learning: what we learn today will help us learn in the future.**

Students and parents will resent even the most relevant and genuine homework assignments if teachers do not evaluate and return the work in a timely manner. For homework to be effective, teachers need to assign and explain it clearly in class and have students begin it so they can monitor students' understanding. Students do not necessarily view homework as a priority, however. Researchers studying students' views report they do not enjoy homework that is boring or "busywork," too easy or too hard, or irrelevant to their lives. When students see homework as intrinsically interesting, they use more homework management strategies, such as self-regulation and self-monitoring (Xu 2007). But what constitutes effective and engaging homework? It appears that optimally designed homework is that which is personally meaningful and enhances both self-efficacy and self-regulation.

Authentic Purpose and Relevance

The quality of homework matters. Homework designed on the basis of best practice is developmentally appropriate and engages students in their own contexts. As Alleman and colleagues (2010) contend, homework that places a premium on authentic learning—learning that emphasizes tasks that integrate and transfer knowledge to the real world—has the most impact. Homework assignments, scholars argue, stand to be most genuine when they ask students to solve real, relevant problems (Newman 1996, in Alleman et al. 2010).

Meaningful homework integrates students' family and community and is strengths-based. A recent review (Alleman et al. 2010) offers key suggestions: for example, a science unit on the importance of conservation will be more meaningful when tied to assignments that ask students to gather, compare, and debate data from their communities about nonrenewable resources and renewable energy efforts. Student diversity is a tremendous advantage, because students can incorporate data with which they are most familiar into the knowledge of the classroom as a whole. For example, variations in what constitutes a family can be studied and understood in the context of different ethnic and cultural beliefs, allowing students to appreciate the nuances of independent versus interdependent societies.

Homework assignments can also foster a deeper understanding of students' daily lives. A literacy unit on the media might focus on how advertising influences consumer behavior. Alleman and colleagues (2010) suggest that students keep a log of ads they regularly see on television, social media sites, and public transportation; analyze persuasion techniques; and develop a workshop on how to identify the "tricks of the trade." Homework that is contextualized is most likely to attract and retain student interest.

Autonomy

Homework should foster a sense of *ownership*. Teachers can accomplish this by allowing students a measure of autonomy. Perceived autonomy is central to intrinsic motivation and has a profound influence on engagement and academic achievement (Ryan and Deci 2006). Students need to realize that some homework will, by necessity, seem boring. For example, mastery of mathematical concepts demands they be practiced over and over again. Rather than prescribe a way to learn multiplication tables, students may be asked to determine the method that works best for them. Students are more likely to feel engaged when reading and to read for longer periods when they are given the choice of what to read (Schiefele et al. 2012; Wigfield, Gladstone, and Turci 2016).

> In Section 3, page 68, Kathy offers further support of choice in reading and specific practices to foster reading engagement.

The Discourse Against Homework: Concerns and Solutions

Advocates for the reduction or elimination of homework have raised substantive concerns about the quality of homework assignments, as well as the stress it imposes on children and their families, the ways in which it can interfere with family time and extracurricular activities, and the inherent inequity of assigning homework to children who may not have access to help at home (Kohn 2006; Kralovec and Buell 1991). I take up each of these concerns next.

There is no doubt that quality of homework matters. As I described above, well-designed homework is developmentally appropriate and engages students in their own contexts. As Alleman and colleagues

(2010) have argued, homework that places a premium on authentic learning can be most impactful. With its emphasis on engagement in tasks that can promote the integration and transfer of knowledge into real-world settings, authentic learning is genuine, not contrived to fit a particular learning goal. Homework assignments stand to be most genuine when they involve active strategizing to solve real problems that have relevance to students (Newman 1996, in Alleman et al. 2010).

As Kathy explains in Section 1, many teachers assign homework with the belief that students need practice persevering through tasks they do not enjoy. They see this as key to developing self-regulated strategies. However, self-regulation without engagement does not guarantee learning. We do not want to teach children to be compliant for the sake of compliance, nor do we want children to encounter difficulty for the sake of difficulty. Rather, we want to harness children's interest, and foster persistence, through engaging and meaningful assignments. This does not mean that some aspects of meaningful learning do not have moments that are boring or frustrating. Along the way to mastery, we all experience boredom, difficulty, and from time to time, failure; we also most certainly miss out on more enjoyable activities as well. There is indeed a value cost to prioritizing homework, and as students get older, they will be called upon to delay gratification perhaps more that they would wish to. This is part of the learning process, and it is to be expected. Indeed, all manner of adult work demands persistence in the face of boredom, difficulty, and frustration. A forensic scientist must verify results with repeated tests; a landscape or fashion or visual or graphic or Web designer must draft multiple possibilities and carefully check parameters before submitting a final draft. Sustained effort and persistence are learning virtues, as important to achievement across domains as innate talent (Duckworth et al. 2007).

> **Homework is associated with blind compliance in meaningless tasks. That is not what we're arguing for here, but rather a reimagining of what homework can be.**

As alluded to in the previous section, homework should be assigned and explained in class. Importantly, as a review of research has shown, there is wide consensus that homework should not be assigned as punishment (Marzano and Pickering 2007). Appropriate schoolwide homework practices are not unlike good parenting practices—they should be clear, consistent, firm, but flexible when necessary (Marzano and Pickering 2007).

As I showed previously, it does not appear to be the case that American children in general are overburdened with homework. No teacher would wish for children's well-being to suffer as a result of inappropriately demanding homework assignments. Largely because of this, many teachers have taken to suggesting an appropriate time frame in which they believe a given night's homework can be completed, and recommend that, beyond this suggested time frame, children stop working on the assignment in question. Indeed, teachers review homework the next day and appreciate knowing who may need more scaffolding to move forward.

One of the more prominent, and I believe, insidious justifications for eliminating homework is that it places low-income children at a disadvantage and "punishes students in poverty for being poor" (Kralovek and Buell 2001, 39). There is no doubt that, relative to their more affluent peers, lower-income children have fewer resources at home and are more likely to have parents who may have neither the knowledge nor confidence to help their children with homework. Yet as the research described earlier indicates, parents do not need to actively help their children with homework for them to complete it successfully. The current climate of income inequality and its effects on children's academic outcomes suggests that eliminating homework would serve only to increase achievement and opportunity gaps. More affluent parents would continue to practice what sociologist Annette Lareau (2003) has referred to as "concerted cultivation," supporting their children's education through a variety of enrichment experiences; low-income children would be left further behind (see Reardon

2011). Homework, and support for homework, is one opportunity that schools can provide to ensure educational equity. Schools must, and a great many do, assume much responsibility for providing homework help by supporting parents, offering after-school homework help, and organizing homework hotlines. Of course, homework is just one educational opportunity among many. Many schools are providing in-school and after-school enrichment activities.

Homework: Not the Only Pathway, But an Opportunity

It is evident that further research to demonstrate more than a correlational association between homework and academic achievement is warranted. However, given the nature of the positive findings, the least we should do is use these as an opportunity to consider how we can assign useful homework. Our conversation on homework has been too narrow, focused on whether or not we should assign homework, rather than on *how* we can design engaging homework that fosters interest and learning. In the next section, Kathy carefully considers this question. A critical part of teachers' roles is to provide curated invitations, through homework, that help children view and experience the world more expansively than they would have without teachers' guidance.

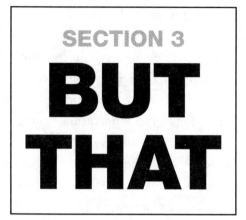

SECTION 3

BUT THAT

Homework Reimagined

KATHY COLLINS

During a summer trip to visit relatives, we sat on the front porch in the light of the long evening watching the kids' frenzied play. It was a moment of perfect playhem (play + mayhem), when one thing flows into another, tree climbing turns into tag, which turns into hide-and-go-seek, which turns into whatever feels like it should be next, and nothing requires an electrical outlet, wifi signal, or adult supervision.

At one point, the kids noticed the faded remains of a hopscotch course spanning the length of the walkway leading from the porch to the street. Its design looked like it was inspired by a Dr. Seuss illustration.

The kids retraced the lines, gathered stones, and played rounds of hopscotch. Someone asked to be timed, and a competition arose. They tried different strategies to hop-skip-jump the fastest, including barefoot trials, starting from the finish line, and decreasing the height of their jumps. They analyzed what part of the course slowed them down. Were they losing time on the one-foot hops? As the kids experimented with different variables, we watched in wonder at how they made something out of what was not much of anything.

Arguments flared as they called each other out for starting before the timekeeper said, "Go!" They established terms of disqualification, including stepping on borders and missing squares altogether. This turn of events and change in tone might sound awful on paper, but the kids were engaged in negotiating the conditions to make this game work. We adults stayed out of it, suppressing our urges to intervene.

For almost an hour, the kids timed each other using decimals and place value, to figure out the time difference between, say, 12.35 seconds and 12.76 seconds. They recorded time trial data in chalk, and calculated their averages. Even though this was a summer scene, their game was infused with evidence of in-school learning, including a variety of math skills, data collection, orchestration of strategies, and task stamina. Yet their work and play from start to finish was self-initiated and self-sustained—no assignment necessary.

At this point, you may be wondering what this lighthearted summer play scene has to do with the hand-wringing topic of homework. Well, that depends on your view of homework. Although this was indeed kids' play, it also contained characteristics of ideal homework based on the research Janine shared in Section 2.

- The children were motivated and engaged.
- The children had agency to initiate, strategize, and problem-solve.
- The tasks were challenging, and the children were enthusiastically taking them on.
- The tasks offered real-life authentic transfer of schoolwork.
- The tasks were inherently differentiated for the different abilities and interests and ages.
- Feedback was immediate, task-based, and resulted in improvement.

- The adults were available, supportive, and positive about the tasks.

By starting Section 3 with a story of children at play rather than an anecdote about children doing a traditional version of homework, my intention is to loosen the hold that homework folders, logs, worksheets, repetitive tasks, drills, and other typical assignments have on our collective vision of children's homework and to move toward a more expansive vision of homework that is research-based yet child-centered, and that is worthy of teachers' and children's time.

In Section 2, Janine indicated that research is not conclusive about whether homework improves elementary school-aged children's academic performance. On the other hand, she also presented research in Section 2, page 27, showing that homework can be a vehicle for fostering adaptive beliefs about learning, especially with regard to the development of self-regulation, perseverance, personal responsibility, and achievement motivation.

For specific research on the value of homework in fostering adaptive learning beliefs

see Section 2, page 27.

Because elementary school homework is but one of the things that may help young children develop these highly functional work habits and pro-learning habits of mind, I'll share homework ideas that are worth it for those reasons, even if the homework doesn't necessarily lead to stronger academic performance. Additionally, in Section 2 Janine provided research showing that choice, motivation, and family support are important aspects of homework, and I'll share suggestions for homework that are considerate of children's (and families') extracurricular lives and interests.

But first, I'd like to make the case that children's self-initiated and engaged play and projects can also do lots of the work of helping children develop strong learning dispositions and that homework can be a vehicle for teachers to learn about children's lives beyond the classroom. When teachers know what children do and care about outside of school, they can provide guidance, support, and authentic feedback and personalized encouragement.

Most families and educators may see the value of children's play before children start school, yet for many it might be hard to trust that children continue to benefit from the pleasure of play over the rigor of assignments and homework once they are school-aged. After all, when a parent sneaks a peek at her son or daughter as they spend hours choreographing and practicing a dance routine to some cloying pop song, it might be hard to see how this will help them attain economic security in their future.

In the absence of traditional kinds of homework, parents might worry whether academic understandings and school performance (and therefore, achievement and ambitions and grades and scores and a prosperous future) will fall through the cracks of the Minecraft landscape that their children spend days creating. Adults may start thinking, "Less play, more work," as their children move through the grades. And teachers who are accountable for scores and data showing academic growth might feel pressured to think the same way as they plan school days with less play and more work.

There are compelling developmental, evolutionary, academic, social, and emotional growth-based rationales for the importance of play for children (Brown and Vaughan 2009) When children are engaged and invested in their play, whether they're building a fort out of pillows, building an animal hospital with little figures and blocks, building a spaceship out of discarded cardboard or building a world in Minecraft, they exhibit characteristics of powerful learners. If we were to observe their play, we would likely find evidence of achievement motivation, stamina, creative strategy use, engagement, transfer, agency, time management, and so on. Teachers can make use of the attributes of children at play by considering alternative visions of what constitutes a homework assignment.

Characteristics of Play That Can Inform Homework Practices

When people are more engaged and motivated there are:

- invitations to make choices and to revise those choices
- possibilities for differentiation to calibrate to strengths, struggles, interests, and resources
- relevance and authentic connections to interests, experiences, goals and desires
- characteristics of mindfulness rather than mindlessness
- feedback and reflection that are meaningful.

These characteristics align with Janine's research findings about homework benefits. With all of this in mind, we'll consider ways to apply these characteristics to an expansive vision of homework, one that is considerate of children's lives outside of school and sensitive to children's needs, strengths, and interests. Additionally, we'll strive to be inclusive of school communities with traditional homework policies and those who have implemented alternatives.

The Importance of Choices— Having Them and Making Them

Peter Johnston's book *Choice Words* (2004) was one of the gateway texts that led many practicing teachers to think about the importance of choice and agency in the classroom. Yet simply giving kids lots of choice among activities and tasks doesn't necessarily lead to intrinsic motivation to act on them. There are ideal conditions for choice that can optimize children's motivation. In the abstract for their article in *Educational Psychology Review*, Idit Katz and Avi Assor write:

> Choice can be motivating when the options meet the students'
> need for autonomy, competence, and relatedness. For example,
> choice is motivating when the options are relevant to the students'

interests and goals (autonomy support), are not too numerous or complex (competence support), and are congruent with the values of the students' culture (relatedness support) (2007).

So where might choices that give children autonomy, a sense of competence, and relevance to their lives come into play with regard to homework? In Section 2, we learned that homework, at its best, should foster a sense of ownership, instill competence, and engage children in their own contexts, so let's explore what that can look like in practice.

Choice Opportunities

A mother of three children, ages eight, ten, and twelve, who attend a school with daily homework assignments, described this scenario:

> Our evenings were predictable. We'd pick up the kids from after school care and activities and scramble to get dinner ready. We'd eat and then it was time for the kids to do their homework. At that time, we'd be on standby to help (or nag) when necessary. Our twelve-year-old headed right to her room to do her homework. She was stressed out about finishing it, especially as it got closer to bedtime. Our ten-year-old worked at the kitchen table because he liked to have someone nearby. Our eight-year-old usually threw some sort of fit, which ranged from silent rage-y behaviors to crying and carrying on. We tried lots of things with her—from ignoring the tantrums to meeting them head on—yell for yell. Nothing worked. Homework was anxiety-producing for everyone.

This mom realized that although it suited the family to have a single homework time frame that took place after dinner, it didn't work for their homework-reluctant youngest child who was often (and under-standably) tired after the long day of school and after-school activities. Homework proponents often claim that homework helps children develop time management skills, but in many households, it's usually the adults who determine the time and place when homework gets done. Elementary school-aged children are not often in charge of setting their own schedules and prioritizing tasks. If helping children manage time is a homework objective, parents might consider releasing control of children's use of time by facilitating experiments and reflections with kids, as this mom did:

> After a couple of weeks of playing around with homework timing, our daughter realized that it was easier for her to do homework during after-school care or right before dinner so that she could have a longer play time afterward. Honestly, there are usually one or two days during the week when she doesn't do her homework at all. We just send in a note to the teacher. Sometimes it's just not worth the battle. We just feel like having down time can be more important at this point. After all, kids work hard all day at school! It's still not smooth sailing, but we don't have daily battles like we used to.

Although this family solved a problem specific to homework timing, the lifelong lesson for their daughter was learning that if something is not working, one can experiment with ways to make it better. In this case, the child tried timing options and made homework fit into her own context. She had a measure of autonomy (with parental support) to figure that out. We support children to develop agency when they can reflect on the demands, limitations, and resources available to help them figure out how to deal with tasks and challenges, whether it's doing homework, gathering their things for soccer practice, or handling any other kind of task.

For children to benefit from homework, they need to become metacognitive about the choices they can make to get homework done.

A secondary benefit of giving children opportunities to determine for themselves their preferences is that it activates the process of self-regulation and ownership ("What do I need to do my best work?" and "How can I make this work?") and the development of positive learning beliefs ("We can figure this out!"), which Janine showed are critical aspects of developing achievement motivation. The self-regulatory process of moving from self-awareness ("This isn't working well"), to identifying possibilities ("Other options might be X, Y, or Z"), to trying them out, and then to reflecting on what works best and using children's preferences to manage their learning or their play is a process that is transferrable to anything children do, whether they're trying to figure out their best conditions for practicing piano, completing their household chores, or finding time to fit in their own passions, pursuits and projects.

Teachers can facilitate conversations among their children and families about homework experiences, inquiring about when they do it, their mood about it, what encourages them, what frustrates them, and use these inquiries to cocreate and communicate clear and tailored homework expectations and possibilities.

Choices About the Content of Homework

"I already know how to do this math! Why do I have to do twenty problems for homework? It's so boring!" Marcus, a fifth grader, complained to his parents. Why, indeed? Four nights a week, Marcus and his classmates had to complete and turn in the same assigned work regardless of their individual strengths, struggles, and situations.

A way to give that kind of assignment a makeover would be to embed more opportunities for Marcus and his classmates to make choices about what to do (Anderson 2016). For example, instead of twenty-five problems, the teacher could assign five problems with a varying range of difficulty and invite the children to select two of them to complete. The teacher might also arrange the problems on the page so they vary between easier and more challenging instead of simply going from the easier ones to harder ones. Recall that in Section 2, Janine explained Harris Cooper's research suggesting that mixing up difficulty levels on homework (difficult problems adjacent to easier ones) is more likely to invite children to choose to take on more challenging work. Perhaps children can be asked to select a problem and follow Joyce Epstein's TIPS protocol described in Section 2.

Another example of content choice is the way Rita assigned homework. During the water study in her class, she asked her students to share the science content they had learned with someone at home. For this particular homework, the only requirements were to use domain-specific vocabulary, to give examples of water in the three states, and to answer the at-home learners' questions.

The children could choose whether they wanted to tell, draw, write, or create a slide presentation to teach the content. Prior to the assignment, Rita and her students brainstormed who they might teach and ideas for how they could present the information at home. It's important to note that Rita had provided opportunities and instructional support for children to try out all of these modes of presentation in the classroom setting and carefully scaffolded the choices to help ensure that students' homework was productive. In school, the children shared how they presented the information at home and compiled a list of questions they received from their families. These questions became the fuel for further inquiry into the topic.

> **Notice that the teacher here provides carefully scaffolded choice to help ensure students' homework is productive.**

It's also worth mentioning that if we're considering the importance of choice and agency, it's possible that some elementary school children and their families might choose *not* to do a homework assignment. If homework is assigned and a child doesn't do it, it's worth investigating the reasons. For example, might it be a content matter (too hard), quantity matter (too much), or time struggle (too busy)? By finding out what is going on at home, the teacher is better able to recalibrate homework content and/or expectations while also using this information to plan instruction during the school day.

Alternatively, the reasons children don't do their homework may be out of their control altogether. For example, children's families may be under economic or emotional duress, the stress of which may impact care-givers' abilities and availability to provide supports for their children's homework. If a teacher or school community has many children for whom support at home is inconsistent or unavailable for whatever reason, it's important that homework assignments are the type that can be completed independent of adult help and that don't require particular materials and resources that may not be accessible in the children's homes.

Perhaps a family prioritizes something else over homework, such as downtime, playtime, family time, or time for other non-school-related activities, like athletics, arts, clubs, or organizations. Again, it's important that the teacher and family communicate about this so that accommo-dations can be made on both the home and school sides. For example, the teacher might send assignments home so that the families can see what the children have been working on in school, whether or not the child completes the assignment. The teacher might also send home in-class work that needs to be finished or prepared, such as final editing of a writing piece in advance of a writing celebration or finishing a lab report about a science experiment, with fair expectations that the child will, indeed, work on it at home. The families, for their part, will agree to support the child to read at home each day and to work on content and learning dispositions that will benefit the child's continued academic, social, and emotional growth.

Elementary school teachers might even consider creating a version of study hall, perhaps something more like a "school–home bridge time." This would require setting aside twenty minutes at the end of the day, perhaps a couple of days a week, for children to work on homework, school/home projects, enrichment activities, skill-supporting practice across content areas, or self-chosen work in efforts to provide children with time, space, materials, and instructional support that can nurture healthy learning dispositions, time management skills, and achievement motivation. Of course, the challenge here is finding those twenty minutes a couple of times a week!

Elementary school-aged children should not face consequences in school, such as loss of recess, choice time, or other highly coveted in-school activities, when they don't do their homework (see Epstein and Van Voorhis 2001). Instead, teachers and children (and families, at times) would be better served by communicating about the situation and collaborating on possible solutions, remedies, or alternatives.

Differentiation and Homework: One Size Can't Fit All

I can understand why this idea—differentiating homework—might give teachers night terrors as they imagine going through the homework life cycle for each child in an effort to create highly customized versions. So let me offer reassurance and comfort: differentiated homework doesn't mean that a teacher creates twenty-five different assignments for each child in his classroom, nor does it mean that a teacher creates Goldilocks homework—hard, medium, and easy versions. Instead, we can imagine differentiable homework, meaning homework that is open-ended and malleable to match a variety of abilities, dispositions, interests, and family cultures. This sort of homework has multiple entry points, and so children (and families) can approach it in a way that matches their needs, strengths, and resources.

Many teachers assign homework as a grid or menu of options that also includes any necessary attachments and materials. The options are relevant to in-school learning and are considerate of children's out-of-school conditions, such as working parents, family language barriers, and after-school activities. This is one example of a teacher providing carefully scaffolded choices that Janine shows research supports in Section 2, page 42.

This is one example of carefully scaffolding choice that Kathy speaks about earlier and that Janine shows research supports in Section 2, page 42.

Sample Homework Grid for Grade 1

Please select FOUR tasks to complete this week. Bring any artifacts to school on Friday, and be ready to share them during our morning meeting.

Play a board game, card game, or video game with someone at home. *(We've been thinking a lot about being a considerate friend to others. See if you can use some of the stuff we learned, like taking turns, compromising, being kind, and so on.)* I played _____ with _____. (Include a photo if you'd like.)	Build or make something (blocks, Legos, food, art, writing, dance routines, and so on). I made_____. (Take a photo or video, make a sketch, or bring in your work to share.)	Free night. No homework. *(Don't forget to read!)*
Do four of the math problems on the attached sheet. Circle the problem that was most challenging for you. Remember: Show your work. Check your work.	We're going to get a new student next week. Ask someone at home to give you two bits of advice for helping our new classmate feel welcome. Be ready to share your advice on Friday during our circle time.	We are looking for signs of spring on our nature walk on Friday. Look out a window at home. Sketch or write about two signs of spring you can see on the attached picture/lined paper.
The poem that we read last week is attached. Read it with someone at home and talk about it. Underline the parts/words that you talked about with someone at home.	Play outside. *(What did you play?)*	We've been thinking about gratitude and the importance of "thank you." Write a thank-you note to someone at school and bring it in to deliver. (Remember to be specific and to use your best handwriting, spelling, and punctuation!)

I read every day at home!

(1) I read by myself. (2) I read to someone. (3) Someone read to me.
(4) How did reading go?

Fri.	Sat.	Sun.	Mon.	Tues.	Wed.	Thurs.

Typically, homework grids include opportunities to practice school learning at home in the children's own contexts, as well as options for free choice and play that enable children to activate self-regulation, perseverance, and problem-solving skills on their own self-chosen activities. PS 118, a public school in Brooklyn, recently implemented an "Exercise Your Brain Menu" approach to homework as described by Albrecht and Zimmer (2016), whose article contains a sample grid from a third-grade classroom.

A powerful attribute of homework grids is that they are highly differentiable for children and their families, too. The tasks reveal the work of the classroom and provide opportunities for children and their caregivers to have interactions about learning as well as conversations about the school day. Furthermore, each task on the grid can be approached in a variety of ways, depending on the child's preferences, strengths, struggles, and resources.

For those considering accountability and feedback, there are multiple ways for children to share what they've done on homework grids, such as creating artifacts, like photographs, sketches, writing, or participating in whole-class or small-group discussions of their work.

Additionally, teachers can "stack" the grids in ways that invite children to work on necessary or vulnerable skills by including options that are relevant to both their lives and their learning needs. Some teachers also leave blank squares for children to create their own tasks and activities.

Relevance: Opportunities to Bridge the Gap Between School Life and Home Life

The following dialogue exchange with children is as common (and as predictable) as a knock-knock joke:

PARENT: How was school today?

CHILD: Boring/fine/okay/good.

PARENT::   What did you do?

CHILD: Nothing.

According to teachers, one of the main reasons for and benefits of assigning homework is that it's an efficient vehicle for sharing information about what children are doing and learning in school. Often, however, this information transfer only goes one way—from school to home. Meanwhile, research shared by Janine in Part 2 suggests the importance of creating homework that's relevant to students' lives, cultures, and community contexts. With this need for relevance in mind, communication transfer needs to work both ways—from school to home *and* from home to school. After all, how can teachers create relevant tasks and tailor meaningful instruction if they don't know much about their students' lives outside of the classroom?

Opening the Lines of Communication Between Home and School

To compensate for the lack of detail that typically characterizes caregiver–child interactions about the school day, teachers assign "tell-about/ask-about" homework.

Tell someone at home about three of these topics:

- the surprise visitor that appeared in our classroom this morning and how we dealt with it

- characteristics of insects, including the names of the three body parts

- ways to add two digit numbers (Make up a problem and show them!)

- something you remember about our meeting with our reading buddies

- something you laughed about today

- something you learned about today

- something you did with a friend today.

Remember to give details and to be specific!

For tell-about homework, children are prompted to talk at home about things that happen during in school. These prompts can be useful scaffolds to help children recall and share information and stories from their school day. This homework is also very timely and nimble because the teacher can tailor the prompts to "hot-off-the-press" curricular content, events, and inquiries.

Teachers have found it helps to take a few minutes at the end of the day to give children a chance to rehearse with a partner how they will share information at home. One fourth-grade teacher even created a brief and informal whole-class inquiry entitled, "How can we tell our school stories so they are interesting to people at home?" Although the short-term intention of this inquiry was to help children to talk about school in engaging ways, the bigger goal was transfer—to support children's oral language development and conversation skills.

An alternative to tell-about homework is to frame it as ask-about homework. This version is often directed to families of younger children, prompting adults to ask about school day topics.

Ask your child:

- about his or her fifth-grade reading buddy and what they did together today
- which picture book by Ezra Jack Keats is her or his favorite and the reasons why
- to show you how to add numbers using the number line at the bottom of this page
- to tell you the story of one thing he or she did outside during afternoon recess.

Reversing the Direction: Bringing Home into School

When teachers invite children's stories and experiences from home into the classroom, they get to know their students more intimately and an interconnectedness is more likely to develop among children. Teachers can tailor instruction, materials, and opportunities so that they're more relevant to children's lives when they know more than the broad strokes about their children's lives. The following are examples of the sorts of homework prompts that bring home into school.

Look Around and Explore Your Life for Signs of School Learning

- Got measurement? Find at least two examples of measuring tools at home. Sketch, list, or take a photo of the measuring tools you find so we can share our findings at school and add them to our Measurement Collection. Have a talk with someone at home about how you might use the measuring tools you've found.

- Study a "character" from your life. Did you realize that we can get to know characters in our lives just like we can know characters in books? Do one of the following:

  - Sketch a character from your life. Include some objects that matter to your character.

  - List some of your character's traits and name some moments that show these traits. You can use a T-Chart like we used in class, if that helps you organize your work. (see attached example.)

Stories and Settings From Home

- We've been thinking a lot about whether or not the character in our read-aloud book is being brave about taking on challenges. Ask a grown-up at home to tell you a story about when he or she was a child and took on a challenge. Remind the grown-up that challenges can be physical (like surviving in a storm), emotional (like tending to a sick pet), or social (like making friends in a new place).

- Weather: Ask someone at home about what they do to find out weather forecasts for our survey about Weather Resources. What part of the forecast does he or she tune into most? Ask if she or he has any questions about the weather that we could add to our inquiry.

- We've been thinking a lot about how to "get into" a book. Think about something you love to do, something you "get really into." What's it feel like? How do you know you're into it?

- We've been thinking about our responsibilities in a classroom community. What about at home? How do we take care of our families, our community at home? Think about chores: What are some jobs you're responsible for doing at home? Make a list of them/sketch them.
- Look around your home. Find three objects that mean a lot to you. Make a sketch or take a photo and jot notes about why these objects matter and consider what they reveal about you. We know that what we care about in our lives can connect us and help us understand each other better.

Children may need modeling and examples to complete assignments like these. Teachers can create their own sample responses and include them in homework as guides, which can also help families envision the task so they can support their children.

Every Monday throughout the year, some of my colleagues and I sent home an assignment asking our first graders to share a story from their weekend. For the first several Mondays, the homework assignment looked something like this:

Sketch a picture of something you did over the weekend.
You can label the picture and write about it.

As the weeks went on, the assignment was amped up to match the kinds of expectations we were growing during writing workshop. By the end of the year, the assignment changed to this:

Write about something you did over the weekend. Include at least three sentences and a sketch. Remember to:
- Write neatly so anyone can read it.
- Check your word wall words to make sure they're spelled correctly.
- Use uppercase letters when necessary and use punctuation.
- Read it to yourself to make sure it says what you want it to say.

Because "write about your weekend" was assigned every Monday, children were habituated to think about it over the weekend, knowing that they had to collect a story to share. One day at dismissal, David's mom told me that they were at the grocery store and someone dropped a gallon of milk and it explosived (his word) all over the floor. David was excited, and said that he wanted to write about it for his Monday homework.

This was years ago. In consideration of the research Janine shared, I would give this homework assignment a makeover in the following ways:

- Instead of assigning it on Monday and making it due on the next day, I would extend it so children have several days to complete it, acknowledging the need for family and timing differentiation.
- I would provide time for children to share their weekend stories through talk or sketching, during morning meeting, in small groups, or during snack time chats as an opportunity for children to rehearse what they might write about as well as expand the audience for their stories, so that they aren't just for me.
- To provide real and timely feedback, I would follow up with the children more, asking them questions about their stories (What did it feel like to meet your baby sister for the first time?), mak-

ing connections between children (Have you talked to Wendell and Cheyenne about this? They also just lost their first tooth!), talking to them about their writing (The way you described your baby sister's soft skin and little body makes me go "Aww!"), being an authentic audience for this work (I admire how you got back up after the big tumble. This is a story that you need to share with the world).

I would open wall space to post and publish this homework and invite children to read and talk about each other's weekends. Children could create connections with each other ("Jadelyn and Mikey both got new kittens!"), realize new ideas we get from each other ("I didn't know that the bike shop had a lady there who teaches you how to fix your chain! I'm going to ask my mom if I can get a lesson, too!"), or share advice ("I'm sorry that your grandma left to go back home. That sounds sad. You know how to feel better? You can send her letters and pictures. That's what I do with my Grammy.").

When children do the sort of homework that invites them to explore their worlds and mine them for connections with what they're learning and for connections with each other, they are more likely to realize the relevance in what they are doing in school. Also, this home-to-school communication enables teachers to understand so much more about children's lives, which helps to create instruction that's more tailored to and considerate of the children in the classroom.

Feedback and Reflection That Are Meaningful to the Teacher and the Learner

In Section 2, Janine shared research suggesting that students and families become frustrated when they perceive that homework doesn't get checked closely. Meanwhile, in Section 1, I reported the challenge that teachers face as they try to find time to offer meaningful feedback on homework.

Crowd-Sourced Homework Review

A few years ago, I observed Kevin Moore at work in his fourth-grade classroom in Austin, Texas. It was first thing in the morning, and he and his students were going over a challenging math problem from the night before. Students worked in small groups as they shared ideas for solving this particular problem. I went from group to group, growing more enchanted by the intensity and enthusiasm of children's participation. Mr. Moore circulated, too, offering support and asking follow-up and go-deeper questions. Although my initial intention in spending the morning in this classroom was to watch a master teacher at work and to observe children talking about their math processes, I ended up thinking a lot about homework and feedback.

Other Homework Feedback Options

Give children/caregivers choice about the part of homework on which they'd like to receive feedback.	Let children and caregivers direct your attention to particular parts of homework—parts that were challenging for them, parts where they took risks, parts where they innovated, and so on.
Make feedback meaningful for both the teacher and the learner.	Use specific feedback to nudge the learner; use feedback opportunities to inform instruction by paying attention to common misconceptions, common understandings, and so on.
Realize feedback and accountability aren't synonymous.	Checking homework to see if it's done is one thing, feedback is another. Feedback is personal, specific, and learner-centered.
Inform families about your feedback policies.	Tell them how and when you'll offer feedback; invite them to direct your attention to parts of their children's homework.

Children received immediate and authentic feedback from Mr. Moore and their classmates, they maintained high levels of engagement as they worked through challenges and explained their thinking, and because they worked in small groups, children were exposed to a variety of ways to think about the same thing. This fifteen minutes in the morning also assured children that doing their homework would matter in the community because Mr. Moore wasn't the only audience for their thinking. Teachers can replicate Mr. Moore's approach by using even a few minutes of their morning meetings for children to problem-solve, discuss, or share responses to homework in small groups or partnerships.

Reading at Home

Research shows (and common sense suggests) that the more you read or are read to, the better you read. Increased exposure to words in print is associated with stronger reading proficiency in terms of comprehension, fluency, and vocabulary acquisition (Anderson, Wilson, and Fielding 1988).

The elementary school day schedule, with its time constraints, curricular demands, increased testing and test preparation, as well as special classes and events, may not always offer children enough minutes or blocks of uninterrupted time for extended reading in school, so most teachers assign daily reading homework in efforts to increase the time children spend reading each day. It's important that reading at home gives children a chance not only to practice reading, but also to grow a self-directed reading life, positive attitudes toward reading, and highly functional reading habits.

Again, Choice Matters

Regardless of the way reading is taught in the classroom, children's reading options in school are usually curated by the teacher. In workshop classrooms, we often guide children toward just-right books, which are at their independent reading levels, or children read books that fit within the confines of a particular unit of study. In guided reading classrooms, teachers select the books children read during small-group instruction. In classrooms with basal reading programs, children read the texts provided by the program. Because children's reading choices are often limited in some way in school, this creates a strong case for letting children choose whatever they want to read at home and for letting them choose how they want to read at home.

For example, a child who is fascinated with sharks might want to read a book full of cool visual features even if she can't read the words. A child who is a strong reader may choose to read easier books, such as *Big Nate*, simply because she enjoys them. A child may want to read a joke and riddle book for the tenth time. A child may choose to read the issue of *Ranger Rick* that had arrived in the mail. A child who is passionate about her fantasy football team might spend time reading online articles about players and analyses of games. If children choose what to read, their motivation is likely to be higher (Gambrell and Marinak 2009).

In addition to choice of titles and types of texts, we can also provide children with choices for how their reading will go. Children benefit when they have daily opportunities to listen to a fluent adult read aloud, even after they can read conventionally (Allington and Gabriel 2012). For this reason, teachers may want to give children daily options to read by themselves, read to someone, read with someone, listen to someone read aloud, or read in any combination of these. It's also worth noting that all reading counts, no matter the language of the text. For instance, if the parents speak Chinese, we encourage them to read aloud in Chinese to their children. If the household has lots of books in Spanish corresponding with the primary home language, we encourage children to read those and to listen to adults read them aloud.

Differentiation Matters

Elementary school children who read willingly and regularly at home probably don't need tightly controlled teacher-assigned reading home-work and logs to initiate their out of school reading. For self-motivated readers, reading homework might simply be a pleasant reminder to read for at least *X* minutes, depending on the age, grade, and time of year. Additionally, reading homework for self-motivated readers can involve helping them set their own goals and create plans for their reading, such as creating their own author studies, reading through particular series, digging into a particular genre, making notebook entries, and so on.

On the other hand, the family of a child who is reluctant to read might need and want the reinforcement of a teacher's assignment to get their child to read. Although assignments from a teacher may get a reluctant reader to read at home, research suggests that completing tasks due to extrinsic motivation may be a shallow and short-term victory (Pink 2009).

It's important that teachers work with reluctant readers and their families to figure out how to spark children's intrinsic motivation to read outside of school, by tapping into the child's passions and interests, vulnerabilities, and strengths and to find ways to make reading time at home pleasurable.

Reading Homework Accountability

Beginning in first grade, my children, like so many, have had to record what they read each night on a reading log. One of my kids reads a lot, and the log was a source of frustration because it couldn't contain his reading. He never knew what title to write because he was often reading several things at once. My other child, a more reluctant reader, would follow the reading log instructions with precision. If the log said, "Read for twenty minutes," he would set the oven timer for twenty minutes. He'd read until the timer went off and stop, regardless of whether he was in the middle of the chapter or the middle of a sentence. "I'm only supposed to read for twenty minutes," he'd say as he began recording the title on his log while we nagged him to finish up the chapter. He wasn't reading for reading's sake. He was reading to complete his log entry.

One vulnerability of reading logs is that when they are used for accountability, they may not serve their purpose at all, simply because log entries can be fudged. On the other hand, some children can't fill them out in a way that represents their reading because their reading lives are too big to reduce to the space of a reading log.

There are ways to give reading logs a makeover so that they serve more than a faux accountability measure. Fifth graders in Diane

Arabian's classroom in Portsmouth, New Hampshire, were thinking about ways to read more at home. For two weeks they logged the amount of time they read outside of school on a reading log designed specifically for this purpose. Diane also filled out her own reading log during that time. At the end of the two weeks, Diane modeled how to study the log to analyze behaviors. Her students looked closely at their logs to determine their average time spent reading and to find patterns about when they read more or less, and then they each set goals for how they'd expand their time spent reading. Diane's reading log experiment had characteristics of data logs in real life—short term, focused, and subject to analysis to set goals and to change behaviors.

At-Home Reading Tied to School Work

Even while encouraging children to build their own reading lives outside of school, there are occasions where children need to do some reading at home to be ready for work in their classroom. For example, many students operate in book clubs within their classrooms, and book club members give each other homework assignments, such as "Read up to Chapter 5 before our book club meeting."

At other times, a class will be involved in a reading unit of study with particular strategy or genre emphasis. At these times, teachers might assign reading homework with more of a sense of mission than simply "Read for X minutes." Instead, for example, a teacher might ask children to track the main characters in their books, both at home and in school, and to be ready to talk about their characters with their reading partners.

When a class is immersed in a project or inquiry, teachers may assign reading at home so that children can prepare for their work in school. For example, when my sons were in third grade, they had to select a famous New Hampshire resident (past or present) and create an exhibit about the person including information, artifacts, and biographical details. They found lots of resources, including articles and videos on the Internet, to augment the texts and materials that were accessible in school.

In my first-grade classroom, children selected topics they wanted to research. I would send home a list of topics that the children chose to study and invite families to share any resources they might have at home to support the researchers. One boy's family had a subscription to an astronomy magazine, so he was excited to bring in a couple of past issues for the "outer space" kids. Another child who went to an obstetrician's appointment with her mom brought in brochures and pamphlets from the office for the children who were studying the human body.

When we consider what and how to assign reading homework, we want to bear in mind the research that Janine shared in Section 2, including the need for autonomy, choice, differentiation, and positive parental involvement.

Homework That Is Informed by Children's Passions and Interests

If teachers don't assign daily homework, some families (and educators) might worry about how children use their time and whether they will lose learning ground without nightly work. "If my kid didn't have homework, she'd be spending her time playing video games or watching television for hours," a parent said (while others nodded in agreement) at a parent workshop. At another school, a teacher said something similar: "It's not like they'd be making art or playing outside in the absence of homework. It would just mean more screen time. And what good is that?"

In *Creating Innovators*, Tony Wagner (2012) traces stories of young adults who achieved success in a variety of fields. Despite their diverse upbringings, the young people he profiled had something in common: rich play histories characterized by purpose and passion. It makes me think of most of my colleagues in education—so many of us recall playing school when we were little; we started babysitting businesses because we loved children, even when we were children ourselves; as teenagers, we lingered in the school supply aisles, preferring to shop for pens, notebooks, and fancy folders over toys, shoes, or the coolest clothes. Often the clues to our adult pursuits hide in the play and passions of our childhood.

Unfortunately, sometimes children's downtime involves self-selected activities that teachers and parents may characterize as mindless. When this is the case, parents might place value on homework simply because it seems to be a superior use of time. But sometimes what may look like mindlessness might actually be characterized by a child's thoughtful engagement and intellectual awakeness. What looks like a passive activity can actually be part of a self-chosen achievement trajectory.

Usman Riaz wanted to learn to play percussive guitar. There were no instructors where he lived in Karachi, Pakistan, so he began watching hours and hours of videos of percussive guitarists. In his case, watching YouTube videos was full of intention. He taught himself percussive guitar and became a world famous performer. I recognize that this might be an extreme example of an achievement trajectory— starting with simply watching videos to studying them to eventually becoming a celebrated expert—but this trajectory is a possible and valuable learning experience even on a smaller scale. The child who loves cooking shows and is allowed to experiment in his own family's kitchen and the child who watches *American Ninja Warrior* and pretends she's one, too, on the local playground are transforming from passive video consumers to goal-setting active learners who have mentors, strategies, and achievement motivation. It's worth differentiating between using screen time passively, as a way of tuning out, or actively, as a way of gaining knowledge or inspiration.

I'm reminded of a talk I attended at a National Council of Teachers of English conference a few years ago. Cornelius Minor and Tim Lopez, from the Teachers College Reading and Writing Project, shared research about the importance of supporting children to be creators, not just consumers, of Internet content, social media, audio/visual entertainment, apps, and games. I would also add that we can support them to be connoisseurs, curators, critics, and comprehenders of content, as well.

Teachers can support and value children's self-initiated pursuits by finding ways to connect them with class work and to value them as self-initiated homework assignments. At the 2016 New England Reading Association conference, Franki Sibberson described how she and her third-grade colleagues implemented a version of "genius hour," in which children gave brief presentations and workshops to each other about their passions and interests. Franki said children created sessions on topics such as Spanish for beginners, making origami animals, tips for braiding hair, all about dinosaurs, and so on. For homework, children planned and prepared how they wanted to present their topic, keeping in mind audience interest, timing, organization, and presentation quality. Similarly, at Academia Cotopaxi in Quito, Ecuador, children prepare and present "inspiration projects" based on topics, hobbies, and activities that interest them. At points during the school year, children present their inspiration projects to their classmates and to the whole school community, as well.

Teachers and children can learn as much about each other as they learn about the content presented while also acquiring important life skills, such as presenting to an audience, sharing passions, prioritizing content, and managing time. What a practical way to bring home into school and to honor children's interests! And through it all, children model for each other the pleasure of having hobbies, interests, and passions; methods for developing expertise; and ways to share and teach.

It's safe to say we all hope that our children (those we teach and those we raise) will grow to be the kinds of adults who strike a healthy work–life balance, who get things done, who prioritize tasks, who stick with something even when it gets tricky, who are intellectually curious and academically inclined, and who believe that they are likely to improve and grow in any domain, activity, task, and relationship if they put in hard work and sincere effort. There are approaches to homework design and content that can help children to develop these dispositions.

What if we create homework that acknowledges, honors, and uses the power generated when children discover and engage in their own passions, activities, and hobbies rather than assign tasks that are removed from children's experiences and decontextualized from their lives? What if we create homework that can morph in ways that meet the wide variety of family cultures, expectations, and time constraints? What if we seek a balance in which there will be days when children may not have any homework (aside from expectations that they are reading at home!) and days when they bring work home from school because it's necessary, not simply because it's a habit of our profession? What if we consider that, just like adults who put in a full day of work, elementary school-aged children, too, need downtime and time for self-driven pursuits after a full day of school (Coppola 2015)?

Janine and I hope that we've given you a research-based rationale and a more expansive view of homework that enables you to envision rich possibilities and meaningful alternatives to worksheets, packets, and tasks that simply occupy children's afterschool time. Homework can be most helpful when it's child-centered, when it enables elementary school children to transfer learning into meaningful contexts, and when it invites caregivers to interact in positive ways with their children's school experiences.

AFTERWORD

ELLIN OLIVER KEENE

Throughout my career as an educator, I've participated in tense conversations about how to make homework more meaningful for kids. I've also walked quickly in the other direction, feigning an urgent meeting on my agenda to *avoid* contentious talk about homework. I've been cornered at social events by parents who, upon learning that I work in schools, share their opinions about the importance of rigorous daily homework ("the kind I had to do") as a sure path to an Ivy league experience for their precious and precocious son or daughter. These interactions generally begin with the words, "Don't you think that homework. . . ." I admit it. I've chickened out. I've said, "Oh, yes," and made my way hastily to pour a glass of wine. I've also read articles that are reposted like crazy on social media calling for an absolute end to homework—yesterday!

Why must we talk in absolute terms about homework? As you now know, having read this book, those days are over. We can now face a group of parents who have "it has to be how it was for me" sentiments and offer, as Nell says in the Introduction, a much more "nuanced" view of homework. We can enter into spirited (or other euphemisms) discussions with colleagues about homework and actually have something practical and research-based to offer as an alternative to mind-numbing practices we've held onto far too long. And, we can get off the hamster wheel of nagging our own kids to "buckle down and get it done so that you can do something interesting"!

Kathy and Janine have shown us how to offer choice in homework (didn't you *love* the homework grid?). They've made us think about how to tie homework to children's passionate interests and refine feedback so that teachers aren't caught in a relentless loop of needing to review homework, putting it off, watching the pile grow, feeling guilty, and ultimately having to decide whether it's worth it to dive in. Not a pleasant choice! And they have anchored our understanding in research so that we're no longer in a place where we have to speculate about what's best for kids.

Indeed, this book is a gift. It is a lively, engaging, often humorous look at ourselves stuck in the groove of a record (remember those?), assigning the same type of homework and dealing with the results or lack thereof. Let's knock the needle to the next groove by sharing this book widely with colleagues and parents! In the dozens of practical, engaging suggestions for making homework truly meaningful and the source of an open conversation between home and school, we've got so much to share, and so many ways to change.

REFERENCES

Albrecht, L., and A. Zimmer. 2016. "Park Slope School Ditches Homework for Play-Based Alternatives." https://www.dnainfo.com/new-york/20161005/park-slope/school-gets-rid-of-homework-value-young-children.

Alleman, J., J. Brophy, B. Knighton, R. Ley, B. Botwinski, and S. Middlestead. 2010. *Homework Done Right: Powerful Learning in Real-Life Situations*. New York: Corwin.

Allington, R., and R. Gabriel. 2012. "Every Child Every Day." *Education Leadership* 69 (6): 10–15.

Anderson, M. 2016. *Learning to Choose, Choosing to Learn: The Key to Student Motivation and Achievement*. Alexandria, VA: ASCD.

Anderson, R., P. T. Wilson, and L. Fielding. 1988. "Growth in Reading and How Children Spend Their Time." *Reading Research Quarterly* 23 (3): 285–303.

Beaton, A., I. Mullis, M. Martin, E. Gonzalez, D. Kelly, and T. Smith. 1996. *Mathematics Achievement in the Middle School Years: IEA's Third International Mathematics and Science Study*. Boston: Boston College, Center for the Study of Testing, Evaluation, and Educational Policy.

Bembenutty, H. 2009. "Self-Regulation of Homework Completion." *Psychology Journal* 6: 138–53.

Bembenutty, H., and B. J. Zimmerman. 2003. *The Relation of Motivational Beliefs and Self-Regulatory Processes to Homework Completion and Academic Achievement*. Paper presented at the American Educational Research Association, Chicago, IL.

Bempechat, J., and D. J. Shernoff. 2012. "Parental Influences on Achievement Motivation and Student Engagement." In *The Handbook of Research on Student Engagement*, edited by S. L. Christenson, A. L. Reschly, and C. Wylie, 315–42. New York: Springer.

Bergman, P. 2015. "Parent-Child Information Frictions and Human Capital Investment: Evidence from a Field Experiment." *CESifo Working Paper Series No. 5391*. Munich: Center for Economic Studies and Ifo Institute.

Biesta, G., M. Priestley, and S. Robinson. 2015. "The Role of Beliefs in Teacher Agency." *Teachers and Teaching* 21 (6): 624–40.

Bigelman, L., and D. S. Peterson. 2016. *No More Reading Instruction Without Differentiation*. Portsmouth, NH: Heinemann.

Boaler, J. 2014. "Research Suggests Timed Math Tests Cause Math Anxiety." *NCTM News & Views* 20 (8): 469–74.

Brock, C. H., D. Lapp, J. Flood, D. Fisher, and K. T. Han. 2007. "Does Homework Matter? An Investigation of Teacher Perceptions About Homework Practices for Children from Nondominant Backgrounds." *Urban Education* 42 (4): 349–72. doi:10.1177/0042085907304277.

Brown, S., and C. Vaughan. 2009. *Play: How It Shapes the Brain, Opens the Imagination, and Invigorates the Soul.* New York: Penguin.

Cobb, C., and C. Blachowicz. 2016. *No More "Look Up the List" Vocabulary Instruction.* Portsmouth, NH: Heinemann.

Comer, J. P. 2005. "The Rewards of Parent Participation." *Educational Leadership* 62 (1): 38–42.

Cooper, H. 1989. *Homework.* White Plains, NY: Longman.

———. 2007. *The Battle Over Homework: Common Ground for Administrators, Teachers, and Parents.* Thousand Oaks, CA: Corwin.

———. 2008. *Effective Homework Assignments Research Brief.* Reston, VA: National Council of Teachers of Mathematics.

Cooper, H., K. Jackson, B. Nye, and J. J. Lindsey. 2001. "A Model of Homework's Influence on the Performance Evaluations of Elementary School Students." *Journal of Experimental Education* 69: 181–99.

Cooper, H., J. J. Lindsey, and B. Nye. 2000. "Homework in the Home: How Student, Family, and Parenting Style Differences Relate to the Homework Process." *Contemporary Educational Psychology* 25: 464–87.

Cooper, H., J. J. Lindsey, B. Nye, and S. Greathouse. 1998. "Relationships Among Attitudes About Homework, Amount of Homework Assigned and Completed, and Student Achievement." *Journal of Educational Psychology* 90: 70–83.

Cooper, H., J. C. Robinson, and E. A. Patall. 2006. "Does Homework Improve Academic Achievement? A Synthesis of Research, 1987–2003." *Review of Educational Research* 76 (1): 1–62.

Cooper, H., and J. C. Valentine. 2001. "Using Research to Answer Practical Questions About Homework." *Educational Psychologist* 36 (3): 143–53.

Coppola, S. 2015. "Four Stories That Homework Tells Children About School Learning, & Life." *My So-called Literacy Life,* December 31. https://mysocalled literacylife.com/2015/12/31/four-stories-that-homework-tells-children-about -school-learning-life/.

Coutts, P. M. 2004. "Meanings of Homework and Implications for Practice." *Theory into Practice* 43 (3): 182–88.

Darling-Hammond, L., and O. Ifill-Lynch. 2006. "If They'd Only Do Their Work!" *Educational Leadership* 65 (5): 8–13.

Duckworth, A. L., C. Peterson, M. D. Matthews, and D. R. Kelly. 2007. "Grit: Perseverance and Passion for Long-Term Goals." *Journal of Personality and Social Psychology* 92 (6): 1087–110.

Dufresne, A., and A. Kobasigawa. 1998. "Children's Spontaneous Allocation of Study Time: Differential and Sufficient Aspects." *Journal of Experimental Child Psychology* 47: 247–96.

Dumont, H., U. Trautwein, O. Ludtke, M. Neumann, A. Niggli, and I. Schnyder. 2012. "Does Parental Homework Involvement Mediate the Relationship Between Family Background and Educational Outcomes?" *Contemporary Educational Psychology* 37: 55–69.

Dumont, H., U. Trautwein, G. Nagy, and B. Nagengast. 2014. "Quality of Parental Homework Involvement: Predictors and Reciprocal Relations with Academic Functioning in the Reading Domain." *Journal of Educational Psychology* 106 (1): 144–161. doi:10.1037/a0034100.

Dweck, C. S., and D. C. Molden. 2005. "Self Theories." In *Handbook of Competence and Motivation*, edited by C. S. Dweck and A. J. Elliot, 122–40. New York: Guilford.

Eccles, J. S., and J. A. Gootman. 2002. *Community Programs to Promote Youth Development*. Washington, DC: National Academy Press.

Elkind, D. 2008. "Can We Play?" *The Greater Good: The Science of a Meaningful Life* (online magazine), March 1. http//greatergood.berkeley.edu/article/item /can_we_play.

Ellis, R. R., and T. Simmons. 2014. *Coresident Grandparents and Their Grandchildren: Population Characteristics 2012*. Washington, DC: U.S. Census Bureau.

Else-Quest, N. M., J. S. Hyde, and A. Hejmadi. 2008. "Mother and Child Emotions During Mathematics Homework." *Mathematical Thinking and Learning* 10: 5–35.

Epstein, J. L. 1995. "School/Family/Community Partnerships: Caring for the Children We Share." *Phi Delta Kappan* 76 (9): 701–12.

Epstein, J. L., and F. L. Van Voorhis. 2001. "More Than Minutes: Teachers' Roles in Designing Homework." *Educational Psychologist* 36 (3): 181–93. doi:10.1207/s15326985ep3603_4.

Fairbanks, E. K., M. Clark, and J. Barry. 2005. "Developing a Comprehensive Homework Policy." *Principal* (Jan/Feb): 36–39.

Fan, H., J. Xu, Z. Cai, J. He, and X. Fan. In press. "Homework and Students' Achievement in Math and Science: A 30-Year Meta-Analysis, 1986–2015." *Educational Research Review*. doi:10.1016/j.edurev.2016.11.003.

Galloway, M., J. Conner, and D. Pope. 2013. "Nonacademic Effects of Homework in Privileged, High-Performing High Schools." *The Journal of Experimental Education* 81 (4): 490–510. doi:10.1080/00220973.2012.745469.

Gambrell, L., and B. Marinak 2009. "Motivation: What the Research Says." Reading Rockets. http://www.readingrockets.org/article/reading-motivation -what-research-says

Gill, B. P., and S. L. Schlossman. 2003. "Parents and the Politics of Homework: Some Historical Perspectives." *Teachers College Record* 105 (5): 846–71.

———. 2004. "Villain or Savior? The American Discourse on Homework, 1850–2003." *Theory into Practice* 43 (3): 174–81.

Gill, B., and S. Schlossman. 1996. "'A Sin Against Childhood': Progressive Education and the Crusade to Abolish Homework, 1887–1941." *American Journal of Education* (November): 33.

Gillen-O'Neel, C., V. W. Huynh, and A. J. Fuligni. 2013. "To Study or to Sleep? The Academic Costs of Extra Studying at the Expense of Sleep." *Child Development* 84 (1): 133–42.

Gilliland, K. 2007. "Families Ask: Homework: Practice for Students or a Snack for the Dog?" *Mathematics Teaching in the Middle School* 8 (1): 36–37.

Gladwell, M. 2008. *Outliers: The Story of Success.* New York: Little, Brown.

Glover, M. 2015. "Reconsidering Readiness." *In The Teacher You Want to Be,* edited by M. Glover and E. O. Keene, 160–75. Portsmouth, NH: Heinemann.

Grolnick, W. S., and M. L. Slowiaczek. 1994. "Parents' Involvement in Children's Schooling: A Multidimensional Conceptualization and Motivational Model." *Child Development* 65 (1): 237–52.

Hattie, J. 2012. *Visible Learning for Teachers: Maximizing Impact on Learning.* New York: Routledge.

Hong, E., R. M. Milgram, and L. L. Rowell. 2004. "Homework Motivation and Preference: A Learner-Centered Homework Approach." *Theory into Practice* 43 (3): 197–204.

Hoover-Dempsey, K. V., O. C. Bassler, and R. Burrow. 1995. "Parents' Reported Involvement in Students' Homework: Strategies and Practices." *The Elementary School Journal* 95 (5): 435–50.

Hoover-Dempsey, K. V., A. C. Battiato, J. M. Walker, R. P. Reed, J. M. DeLong, and K. P. Jones. 2001. "Parental Involvement in Homework." *Educational Psychologist* 36 (3): 195–209.

Jeynes, W. H. 2010. "The Salience of the Subtle Aspects of Parental Involvement and Encouraging That Involvement: Implications for School Based Programs." *Teachers College Record* 112 (3): 747–74.

Jimenez-Silva, M., and K. Olson. 2012. "A Community of Practice in Teacher Education: Insights and Perceptions." *International Journal of Teaching and Learning in Higher Education* 24 (3): 335–48.

Johnston, P. 2004. *Choice Words*. Portland, ME: Stenhouse Publishers.

Jones, R. D., and C. Ross. 1964. "Abolish Homework: Let Supervised Schoolwork Take Its Place." *The Clearing House: A Journal of Educational Strategies, Issues and Ideas* 39 (4): 206–209.

Katz, I., and A. Assor. 2007. "When Choice Motivates and When It Does Not." *Educational Psychology Review* 19: 429–42. doi:10.1007/s10648-006-9027-y

Kohn, A. 2006. *The Homework Myth: Why Our Kids Get Too Much of a Bad Thing*. Cambridge, MA: Da Capo Lifelong Books.

Kralovec, E., and J. Buell. 2001. "End Homework Now." *Educational Leadership* (April): 39–42.

Lareau, A. 2003. *Unequal Childhoods: Class, Race, and Family Life*. Berkeley, CA: University of California Press.

Li, J., S. D. Holloway, J. Bempechat, and E. Loh. 2008. "Building and Using a Social Network: Nurture for Low-Income Chinese American Adolescents' Learning." *New Directions for Child and Adolescent Development*, 121: 9–25. doi:10.1002 cd220.

Macnamara, B., D. Z. Hambrick, and F. L. Oswald. 2014. "Deliberate Practice and Performance in Music, Games, Sports, Education, and Professions: A Meta-Analysis." *Psychological Science* 25 (8): 1608–18.

Mapp, K. L., V. R. Johnson, C. S. Strickland, and C. Meza. 2008. "High School Family Centers: Transformative Spaces Linking Schools and Families in Support of Student Learning." *Marriage and Family Review* 43(3/4): 338–68.

Marzano, R. J., and D. J. Pickering. 2007. "The Case for and Against Homework." *Educational Leadership* 46 (6): 74–79.

MetLife. 2007. *The MetLife Survey of the American Teacher: The Homework Experience-A Survey of Students, Teachers, and Parents*. New York: MetLife, Inc.

Muhlenbruck, L., H. Cooper, B. Nye, and J. J. Lindsey. 2000. "Homework and Achievement: Explaining the Different Strengths of Relation at the Elementary and Secondary School Levels." *Social Psychology of Education* 3: 295–317.

National Assessment of Education Progress. 2013. *Digest of Education Statistics*, Table 221-30. Washington, DC: U.S. Department of Education, Institute of Education Sciences, National Center for Education Statistics.

National Center for Educational Statistics. 2011. *America's Youth: Transitions to Adulthood*. Washington, DC: U.S. Department of Education.

Núñez, J. C., N. Suárez, P. Rosário, G. Vallejo, R. Cerezo, and A. Valle. 2015. "Teachers' Feedback on Homework, Homework-Related Behaviors, and Academic Achievement." *The Journal of Educational Research* 108 (3): 204–16. doi:10.1080/00220671.2013.878298.

Özcan, Z. Ç., and E. Erktin. 2015. "Enhancing Mathematics Achievement of Elementary School Students Through Homework Assignments Enriched with Metacognitive Questions." *EURASIA Journal of Mathematics, Science & Technology Education* 11 (6): 1415–27.

Palmer, J., and M. Invernizzi. 2014. *No More Phonics and Spelling Worksheets.* Portsmouth, NH: Heinemann.

Patall, E. A., H. Cooper, and J. C. Robinson. 2008. "Parent Involvement in Homework: A Research Synthesis." *Review of Educational Research* 78 (4): 1039–101. doi:10.3102/0034654308325185.

Pink, D. 2009. *Drive: The Surprising Truth About What Motivates Us.* New York: Riverhead Books.

Pomerantz, E. M., W. Grolnick, and C. Price. 2005. "The Role of Parents in How Children Approach Achievement: A Dynamic Process Perspective." In *Handbook of Competence and Motivation*, edited by A. J. Elliot and C. S. Dweck, 229–78. New York: Guilford.

Pomerantz, E. M., E. A. Moorman, and S. D. Litwack. 2007. "The How, Whom, and Why of Parents' Involvement in Children's Academic Lives: More Is Not Always Better." *Review of Educational Research* 77 (3): 373–410. doi: 10.3102/003465430305567.

Pomerantz, E. M., F. F. Ng, and Q. Wang. 2006. "Mothers' Mastery-Oriented Involvement in Children's Homework: Implications for the Well-Being of Children with Negative Perceptions of Competence." *Journal of Educational Psychology* 98 (1): 99–111.

Protheroe, N. 2009. "Good Homework Policy." *Principal* 89 (1): 42–45.

Ramdass, D., and B. J. Zimmerman. 2011. "Development of Self-Regulation Skills: The Important Role of Homework." *Journal of Advanced Academics* 22 (2): 194–218.

Reardon, S. F. 2011. "The Widening Academic Achievement Gap Between Rich and Poor: New Evidence and Possible Explanations." In *Whither Opportunity? Rising Inequality, Schools, and Children's Life Chances*, edited by G. J. Duncan and R. J. Murnane, 91–115. New York: Russell Sage Foundation.

Rosário, P., J. C. Núñez, G. Vallejo, J. Cunha, T. Nunes, R. Mourão, and R. Pinto. 2015. "Does Homework Design Matter? The Role of Homework's Purpose in Student Mathematics Achievement." *Contemporary Educational Psychology* 43: 10–24. doi:http://dx.doi.org/10.1016/j.cedpsych.2015.08.001.

Rosenthal, R. 2002. "The Pygmalion Effect and Its Mediating Mechanisms." In *Improving Academic Achievement: Impact of Psychological Factors on Education*, edited by J. Aronson, 25–36. San Diego, CA: Academic Press.

Ryan, R. M., and E. L. Deci. 2006. "Self-Regulation and the Problem of Human Autonomy: Does Psychology Need Choice, Self-Determination, and Will?" *Journal of Personality* 74 (6): 1557–86.

Schiefele, U., E. Schaffner, J. Möller, and A. Wigfield. 2012. "Dimensions of Reading Motivation and Their Relation to Reading Behavior and Competence." *Reading Research Quarterly* 47 (4): 427–63. doi:10.1002/rrq.030.

Schmitz, B., and F. Perels. 2011. "Self-Monitoring of Self-Regulation During Math Homework Behaviour Using Standardized Diaries." *Metacognition and Learning* 6 (3): 255–73. doi:10.1007/s11409-011-9076-6.

Shernoff, D. J., and D. L. Vandell. 2007. "Engagement in After-School Program Activities: Quality of Experience from the Perspective of Participants." *Journal of Youth and Adolescence* 36 (7): 891–903. doi:10.1007/s10964-007-9183-5.

Silinskas, G., N. Kiuru, K. Aunola, M.-K. Lerkkanen, and J.-E. Nurmi. 2015. "The Developmental Dynamics of Children's Academic Performance and Mothers' Homework-Related Affect and Practices." *Developmental Psychology* 51 (4): 419–33. doi:10.1037/a0038908.

Silinskas, G., P. Niemi, M. Lerkkanen, and J. Nurmi. 2013. "Children's Poor Academic Performance Evokes Parental Homework Assistance—But Does It Help?" *International Journal of Behavioral Development* 37 (1): 44–56.

Stevenson, H., C. Chen, and S. Lee. 1993. "Mathematics Achievement of Chinese, Japanese, And American Children: Ten Years Later." *Science* 259: 53–58.

Stoeger, H., and A. Ziegler. 2008. "Evaluation of a Classroom Based Training to Improve Self-Regulation in Time Management Tasks During Homework Activities with Fourth Graders." *Metacognition and Learning* 3 (3): 207–30. doi:10.1007/s11409-008-9027-z.

Trautwein, U., and O. Ludtke. 2007. "Students' Self-Reported Effort and Time on Homework in Six School Subjects: Between Student Differences and Within Student Variation." *Journal of Educational Psychology* 99 (2): 432–44.

Trautwein, U., A. Niggli, I. Schnyder, and O. Ludtke. 2009. "Between-Teacher Differences in Homework Assignments and the Development of Students' Homework Effort, Homework Emotions, and Achievement." *Journal of Educational Psychology* 101 (1): 176–89.

Valle, A., B. Regueiro, J. C. Núñez, S. Rodríguez, I. Piñeiro, and P. Rosário. 2016. "Academic Goals, Student Homework Engagement, and Academic Achievement in Elementary School." *Frontiers in Psychology* 7 (463): 1–10. doi: 10.3389/fpsyg.2016.00463.

Van Voorhis, F. L. 2011. "Adding Families to the Homework Equation: A Longitudinal Study of Mathematics Achievement." *Education and Urban Society* 43 (3): 313–38.

Vatterott, C. 2010. "5 Hallmarks of Good Homework." *Educational Leadership* 68 (1): 10–15.

Wagner, T. 2012. *Creating Innovators: The Making of Young People Who Will Change the World.* New York: Scribner.

Walker, J. M., K. Hoover-Dempsey, C. L. Ice, and M. C. Whitaker. 2009. "Parental Involvement Supports Better Student Learning." In *International Perspectives on Student Outcomes and Homework*, edited by R. Deslandes, 25–38. New York: Taylor and Francis.

Warkentien, S., M. Fenster, G. Hampden-Thompson, and J. Walston. 2008. *Expectations and Reports of Homework for Public School Students in the First, Third, and Fifth Grades.* Washington, DC: Institute of Education Sciences, U.S. Department of Education.

Watkins, P. J., and D. W. Stevens. 2013. "The Goldilocks Dilemma: Homework Policy Creating a Culture Where Simply Good Is Just Not Good Enough." *The Clearing House: A Journal of Educational Strategies, Issues and Ideas* 86 (2): 80–85.

Weiner, B. 2005. "Motivation from an Attributional Perspective and the Social Psychology of Perceived Competence." In *Handbook of Competence and Motivation*, edited by A. J. Elliot and C. S. Dweck, 73–84. New York: Guilford.

Wigfield, A., J. Gladstone, and L. Turci. 2016. "Beyond Cognition: Reading Motivation and Reading Comprehension." *Child Development Perspectives* 10 (3): 190–95. http://doi.org/10.1111/cdep.12184.

Xu, J. 2007. "Middle School Homework Management: More Than Just Gender and Family Involvement." *Educational Psychology* 27 (2): 173–89.

Xu, J., and L. Corno. 1998. "Case Studies of Families Doing Third Grade Homework." *Teachers College Record* 100 (2): 402–36.

———. 2003. "Family Help and Homework Management Reported by Middle School Students." *The Elementary School Journal* 103 (5): 503–19.

Xu, J., and H. Wu. 2013. "Self-Regulation of Homework Behavior: Homework Management at the Secondary School Level." *Journal of Educational Research* 106 (1): 1–13.

Xu, J., and R. Yuan. 2003. "Doing Homework: Listening to Students', Parents', and Teachers' Voices in One Urban Middle School Community." *School Community Journal* 13 (2): 25–44.

Zimmerman, B. J., and D. H. Schunk. 2011. "Self-Regulated Learning and Performance: An Introduction and Overview." In *Handbook of Self-Regulated Learning and Performance*, edited by B. J. Zimmerman and D. H. Schunk, 1–2. New York: Routledge.

Look for these other titles in the Not This, But That Series

edited by Nell K. Duke and Ellin Oliver Keene

No More Independent Reading Without Support

Debbie Miller and Barbara Moss

Grades K-6 / 978-0-325-04904-5 / 96pp

No More Reading for Junk

Barbara Marinak and Linda Gambrell

Grades K-5 / 978-0-325-06157-3 / 96pp

No More Summer-Reading Loss

Carrie Cahill, Kathy Horvath, Anne McGill-Franzen, and Richard Allington

Grades K-8 / 978-0-325-04903-8 / 96pp

DEDICATED TO TEACHERS **Heinemann.com**

  @HeinemannPub